SOCIAL, PSYCHOLOGICAL AND SITUATIONAL FACTORS IN WIFE ABUSE

By Kathleen H. Hofeller

PALO ALTO, CALIFORNIA

Published by

R & E RESEARCH ASSOCIATES, INC.
936 Industrial Avenue
Palo Alto, California 94303

Library of Congress Card Catalog Number
81-83618

I. S. B. N.
0-88247-620-3

TABLE OF CONTENTS

LIST OF TABLES

Table | Page

CHAPTER I

HISTORICAL PRECEDENTS FOR WIFEBEATING

Wifebeating has been an accepted practice in Western culture since the early Middle Ages (Gies, 1978). In fact, it is only recently that society has begun to challenge the long standing tradition which gives a man both the moral and legal right to batter his spouse. In order to fully understand the nature of domestic violence, it is necessary to consider wifebeating with regard to both the social context in which it presently occurs, and also in terms of historical precedent.

Because the scope of this study does not allow for an exhaustive history of domestic violence, this discussion will be confined to selected legal, economic, religious, and cultural factors which have in the past contributed to the incidence of wife abuse. For example, wifebeating may be perpetuated by statutes which sanction violence against women or which prohibit them from taking legal action against their husbands. Women who are denied full economic opportunities find it harder - if not impossible - to survive financially without a husband, and religions which view woman's subordinate position as divinely ordained make social change and progress difficult. Finally, cultural conceptions of femininity not only influence the relative overall social status of women, but also effectively control behavior through the process of socialization; women who are brought up to believe that they are weak, incompetent, and helpless are less likely to challenge existing restrictions.

The Middle Ages

During the Middle Ages the influence of Christianity should have theoretically improved the status of women; Jesus' teachings were egalitarian and did not contain the misogyny found in Judaism (O'Faolain, 1973, p. 128). However, the writings of the early saints reflected a basic mistrust of women (Gies, 1978). There were at least two major reasons for the Medieval Church's negative attitudes toward women. First, the Christian religion had incorporated many Jewish beliefs about the nature of the female sex. For example, the narrative of "The Fall" presented a rather uncomplimentary image of woman. To begin with, it was made clear that Eve was entirely to blame for the fact that mankind no longer lived in the idyllic Garden of Eden. During the Middle Ages this was loosely interpreted as meaning that woman was responsible for all the evil and sin in the world (Gies, 1978). In addition, woman's subordinate social position was justified because of her transgression. Furthermore, this submission was a divine commandment, and was therefore less open to question by mortals. Finally, woman was depicted as a creature of guile since it was she who tempted Adam to disobey God. It is worth noting that Adam himself expressed no real responsibility for his own actions, explaining that, "The woman whom thou gavest to be with me, she gave me fruit of the tree and I ate" (Genesis 3:12). Presumably, Adam, too, possessed free will, and certainly could have refused the offer. But, then, that is not the "stuff"of which patriarchies are made.

The extreme asceticism of the Church founders also resulted in a certain amount of prejudice against women (Gies, 1978). Women were seen primarily as a temptation to man to succumb to his carnal desires, thereby impeding his spiritual growth. Given the presence of this asceticism, it is not surprising to find that the writings of such men as Saint Paul reflected an ambivalence toward women. For example, in Galatians Saint Paul stated, "There is neither Jew nor Greek, there is neither bond nor free, there is neither male nor female: for ye are all one in Christ Jesus" (3:28). In Ephesians, however, he wrote, "Wives, be subject to your husbands, as to the Lord. For the husband is the head of the wife as Christ is the head of the Church, its body, and is Himself its Savior. As the Church is subject to Christ, so let wives also be subject in everything to their husbands" (5:22-3).

The feelings about women expressed by early saints were echoed by the clergy of the high Middle Ages. For example, Marbode, an eleventh century bishop, said this of women, "Of all the numberless snares that the crafty enemy [the devil] spreads for us. . .the worst. . .is woman, sad stem, evil root, vicious fount. . .honey and poison" (Gies, 1978, p. 38).[1] However, at least one historian has pointed out that such passages can be misleading unless one closely examines the context in which they were written. Gies (1978) has noted that Marbode's diatribe was primarily in reference to prostitutes, and that when speaking of the matron, this bishop changed his language considerably. In one instance, for example, he named an honor role of women from the Old Testament and early Christian saints and further declared that, ". . .the worst woman who ever lived does not compare with Judas and the best man does not equal Mary" (Gies, 1978, p. 39).[2] In general, however, the Church viewed women as basically simple creatures, ordinarily incapable of higher spiritual or intellectual achievement. Women were weak, both physically and morally, and therefore were justly placed under the total control of their fathers and husbands

(Gies, 1978).

But if the Church were somewhat equivocal in assessing the relative value of the female sex, there was little doubt in the mind of the clergy that a husband had a right, indeed sometimes even an obligation, to beat his wife. For example, a Theological Encyclopedia (circa 1300) compiled by a Dominican monk stated, "A man may chastise his wife and beat her for her correction; she is of his household, and therefore the lord may chastise his own"(Coulton, 1955, p. 615).[3] But it was not only a man's right to correct and control his wife - it was also his duty. Consider, for example, the advice given to husbands by Friar Cherubino of Siena. In his "Rules of Marriage" the husband is told that if verbal correction of a wife does not produce the desired results, then he should ". . .take up a stick and beat her soundly, for it is better to punish the body and correct the soul than to damage the soul and spare the body. . .then readily beat her, not in rage, but out of charity and concern for her soul, so that the beating will rebound to your merit and her good" (Cherubino, 1973, p. 177). Just how many women were bruised and battered out of their husbands' sense of Christian charity and duty, we will never know.

The Medieval Church's attitude toward women, however, was not entirely negative. Although a single woman was still not considered to have been made in the image of God, at least she was viewed as a separate personality in possession of a soul worth saving. Furthermore, woman's status was somewhat improved by the fact that the Church saw marriage as a sacrament instituted by Christ, and taught that a woman was indeed created to be man's helpmate (Gies, 1978). In addition, there were some clerics who disapproved of violence, and spoke out strongly against it (Coulton, 1955, p. 614). Nevertheless, the consensus among the clergy was that a husband had the right to use force against his wife.

The subjection of women to physical abuse was also sanctioned by secular institutions. For example, one thirteenth century French law code stated that, "In a number of cases men may be excused for the injuries they inflict on their wives, nor should the law intervene. Provided he neither kills nor maims her, it is legal for a man to beat his wife if she wrongs him" (Gies, 1978, p. 46). In addition, the laws of Gascony during the Middle Ages included the following statute: "Every inhabitant of this village has the right to beat his wife provided that death does not follow" (Coulton, 1955, p. 617).[4]

Although wives were not protected by law from violence, they did have some legal rights. In both England and on the Continent, women, married or single, could hold land, own goods, make wills, contracts, sue and be sued, and plead in the law courts (Gies, 1978). Women could also inherit estates and titles (Coulton, 1955, p. 617). However, in the eyes of the law, women were still subject to their husbands in most areas. A woman's husband was her lord in every sense of the word. In addition, although women were sometimes allowed recourse through the courts, they were by no means full citizens. In most cases, a woman was not allowed to appear in court on her own, requiring the presence of her husband if any legal action were to be taken (O'Faolain, 1973, p. 145).

During the Middle Ages, the nobility had conflicting norms regarding the proper treatment of women. The Chivalric code admonished men to serve and honor all women and to spare no pain or effort in their service (Gies, 1978), but physical abuse of women in the upper class was also acceptable. For example, consider the "Book of the Knight of La Tour-Landry," a very popular manual, which described the duties and customs of upper class society. In this book, the knight tells his daughters of a wife who once scolded her husband in public. That action made him angry, so he ". . .smote her with his fist down to the earth and then with his foot struck her in the face and broke her nose which all of her life after she had her nose crooked." This injury ". . .shent and disfigured her visage after, for that she might not for shame show her visage, it was so foul blemished" (Coulton, 1955, p. 617).[5] In addition, wives had far less freedom in their love affairs than did their husbands. Men from all social classes customarily had mistresses, and this practice was generally condoned. However, if a woman dared commit adultery - and was caught at it - she was publicly disgraced and her lover could be castrated or killed. During the thirteenth century in Spain, a husband or fiance could kill the woman or her lover without fear of any legal retribution (Gies, 1978).

The societal view of lower class women appears to have been more uniformly unflattering. In the earthy "fabliaux," short stories about peasant life, these wives were depicted as both adulterous and treacherous. These women were usually ill-tempered shrews, dedicated to making the lives of their husbands miserable (Gies, 1978, p. 45). It is important to note that in these accounts, the man usually becomes so frustrated with his wife that he occasionally beats her. However, the tales also imply that the last word is always hers and that somehow the beatings had little effect on her behavior. This stereotype of the scolding wife provoking her husband to violence justly deserved is a myth which still exists today.

Generally speaking, medieval society viewed women as little more than overgrown children, and occasionally troublesome creatures in need of strict control: "The female is an empty thing, easily swayed: she runs great risks when she is away from her husband. Therefore, keep females in the house, keep them as close to yourself as you can, and come home often to keep an eye on your affairs and to keep them in fear and trembling. . . If you have a female child, set her to sewing and not to reading, for it is not suitable for a female to know how to read unless she is going to be a nun. . ." (Paolo da Certaldo, 1973, p. 169).

Although women had almost no political power, and limited legal power, they were active in industry, and the growth of towns tended to increase women's freedoms. For example, many women were traders and were an important part of the industrial life of London. Women were prominent in cloth making, in the twenty-five crafts associated with cloth making, and in silk making. Guilds ordinarily allowed female members. However, then as now, women were ordinarily paid less for the same work than men (Coulton, 1955, p. 619). Nevertheless, during the Middle Ages a woman's "sphere" frequently included activities in industry and production, and her labors could often net substantial income. In the area of economics, women were considered to be productive, valuable members of society.

Even so, life for the Medieval woman was primarily one of subjection to the male members of her family. Although society was slowly beginning to grant her some rights and privileges, she was still provided little, if any, protection from a violent spouse.

Renaissance and Reformation (1400 to 1700)

The Renaissance and Reformation were both periods of extraordinary social, political, and religious change. The status of women was changing, too. Women were no longer considered to be merely chattel; for the first time higher education was advocated for women, although initially only for those of the upper class (Camden, 1952). However, there was still some uncertainty regarding a woman's proper role. The

Elizabethan wife was, "A curious mixture of slave and companion, a necessary evil, and a valued lieutenant" (Camden, 1952, p. 148). According to custom, a wife's primary duty was subjection to her husband. She was always to acknowledge herself as an inferior, and be ready at the beck and call of her spouse. The first duty of a husband was to love his wife, and to govern her or rule her, and to always maintain himself in the superior position which God intended him to occupy (Camden, 1952).

A more intimate view of married life during the Renaissance is provided by a fourteenth century Florentine merchant, whose diary described the type of relationship which he developed and maintained with his wife. For example, the author mentioned that he kept all his private papers locked away, and was careful to express disapproval of "bold females" who tried to know about things outside the house. Furthermore, he took pains to maintain his dominance at all times. "Never, at any moment, did I choose to show in word or action the least self-surrender in front of my wife. I did not imagine for a moment that I could hope to win obedience from one to whom I had confessed myself a slave. Always, therefore, I showed myself virile and a real man" (Alberti, 1973, p. 189). But perhaps the most telling view of woman's proper role as a wife can be found in a woodcutting made during the fifteenth century. It is entitled "The Manwoman" and the woodcutting depicts a woman sitting on the back of a man pulling him by the hair and beating him with a stick (Camden, 1952, p. 25).

The Protestant Reformation brought both progress and problems for women. On the one hand, there was a revitalized emphasis on the dignity and spirituality of marriage. Furthermore, a couple was justified in seeking a divorce if their relationship did not allow for the spiritual growth of both people. For example, one Dominican monk wrote that,

"In all things that pertain to salvation, one should have as much regard for a woman as for a man. For though she is bound to keep her place, to put herself under the authority of her husband. . .her subjection does not cancel the right of an honest woman, in accordance with the laws of God, to have recourse to and demand, by legitimate means, deliverance from a husband who hates her. For the Lord has certainly not made married woman subservient to have her be polluted and tormented by the extortions and injuries of her husband. . .a wife is not so subject to her husband that she is bound to suffer anything that he may impose upon her" (Bucer, 1973, p. 201). In practice, however, obtaining a divorce either through civil courts or through the Church was extremely difficult, and conditions did not substantially improve for several hundred years. In addition, even in the new Protestant sects, women were not allowed a high degree of authority. For instance, although Luther wrote articles in defense of women, he also said, "Men have broad shoulders and narrow hips, and accordingly they possess intelligence. Women have narrow shoulders and broad hips. Women ought to stay at home; the way they were created indicates this, for broad hips and a wide fundement to sit upon, keep house and bear and raise children" (Luther, 1973, pp. 196-197). In short, neither Catholic nor Protestant leadership was yet ready to grant women full equality with men.

Although women were allowed to become involved in new activities and have a certain degree of freedom during the Renaissance and Reformation, the reaction to these changes was not entirely supportive. In 1620, for example, King James became so annoyed at the presumption of women to copy men's dress and to cut their hair, that he urged the clergy to take the matter promptly in hand. Not surprisingly, the impropriety of women who would take on men's clothes - and men's roles - soon became the topic of sermons throughout England. The man-woman who adopted masculine dress became an object of great concern and derision (Camden, 1952, p. 163).

Perhaps the most disturbing and malevolent phenomenon during the sixteenth and seventeenth centuries was witch-hunting. It has been suggested that some of the anti-feminism of these witch hunters was a reaction to the growth of women's rights which had been occurring (O'Faolain, 1973, p. 207). The most authoritative work on demonology, the "Maleus Maleficarum," was written about 1486 in Germany. By 1520 the book had gone through fourteen known editions. According to this book, women were more likely to be seduced by the devil because they were feeble both in mind and body. Women were described as being incapable of attaining the level of intellectual understanding of spiritual values which men could achieve. However, the "natural" reason for women to become witches was that ". . .she is more carnal than a man as is clear from her many carnal abominations. . . To conclude, all witchcraft comes from carnal lust, which is in women insatiable" (Kramer & Sprenger, 1973, p. 209).

The fear of witches was by no means confined to less educated classes; intelligent, learned men, clergy and lay alike, firmly believed in them. For example, Jean Bodin, a French jurist and political theorist, accepted the existence of witches and even made reference to Eve as the first seducer. According to Bodin, Satan first addressed himself to a woman, and the devil still used women to get at their husbands. Witch hunting peaked in the second half of the sixteenth century, but continued for another one hundred years. Between 1587 and 1593, for instance, twenty-two villages in the region of Trier burned 368 supposed witches. In 1577 alone, Toulouse and its environs reportedly burned 400 innocent women (O'Faolain, 1973, p. 215).

With regard to legal rights, women in the Renaissance were still seen as being totally subject to their husbands' "correction." In England, for example, ". . .if a man beat an outlaw, a traitor, a pagan, his villein, or his wife it is dispunishable because by the Law of Common these persons have no action. God send gently women better sport or better company" (Camden, 1955, p. 116).[6] By the time of King James' reign, (1603 to 1625), some judges had expressed the opinion that a wife might have some recourse against her husband for "unreasonable correction." Under Charles II, Sir Mathew Hale held that moderate castigation was to be understood as meaning a verbal admonition only. However, many jurists still maintained that a husband had a right to beat his wife as long as he did not do it "outrageously." For example, the Common Law of Wales allowed a husband to beat a disrespectful wife three strokes with a rod the length of his forearm and the thickness of his middle finger (Langley & Levy, 1978, p. 48).[7] Finally, in 1632, in a methodical collection of statutes and customs entitled "The Lawes Resolutions of Womens Rights: or, The Lawes Provision for Woemen (sic)," the author's learned opinion was that husbands indeed had the right to beat their wives but, in fact, shouldn't use it (Camden, 1955, p. 116).[8]

As during the Middle Ages, women played an important part in the economy of the Renaissance and Reformation. Trade guilds appear to have been open to girls who had to earn their livelihood, and marriage to a member of a guild conferred rights upon the wife. Furthermore, a woman was able to keep these rights even after her husband's death. Women were also allowed to keep inns and manage ale houses. They worked as upholsterers and milliners and were sometimes paid for being wet, dry, and sick nurses (Camden, 1955).

Therefore, it would appear that during the Renaissance

women who stayed in their proper roles as sober wife or desired lover - when wanted - were treated with some praise and reverence. However, when women tried to take on other responsibilities and roles, they were commonly met with scorn (Camden, 1955, p. 270).

Early Modern Period, England and France (1700 to 1800)

By the beginning of the eighteenth century, women had achieved a number of legal, moral, and spiritual rights. However, the legal theory of the eighteen hundreds would nearly destroy these gains, and in fact leave women with fewer prerogatives than they had enjoyed during the Middle Ages. The cause of this change was the theory known as "couverture." As explained by Blackstone in his *Commentaries on the law of England*, it was a custom or law which held that, "In marriage the husband and wife are one person in law; that is the very being or legal existence of the women is suspended during the marriage, or at least incorporated and consolidated into that of her husband; under whose wing, protection, and cover, she performs everything" (Hymowitz & Weissman, 1978, p. 23).[9] The overall effect of "couverture" was that a married woman could not own property, have money in her name, control her wages if she worked, and could not make contracts or sue or be sued in court (Hymowitz & Weissman, 1978, p. 23). This latter restriction had particular application to domestic violence, because a woman was unable to prosecute her husband for beating her. It was impossible for a person to sue himself, and a wife simply did not exist in the "eyes of the law." With this legal sleight of hand, women were essentially reduced to near slavery once again. Single women, however, were treated more or less like men, since it was reasoned that an unmarried woman needed the protection of the law. With the exception of the right to vote and sit on a jury, a single English woman enjoyed a good deal of freedom, at least by contemporary standards.

Women on the Continent often fared even worse. For example, Napoleon Bonaparte was dedicated to the proposition that men, in fact, possessed their wives. His legislation changed the laws of equality that had been in force during the Revolution, leaving women in the position of having no legal protection whatsoever from their husbands. As Napoleon once told his Council of State, "The husband must possess the absolute power and right to say to his wife: Madam, you shall not go out, you shall not go to the theater, you shall not receive such and such a person; but the children you bear shall be mine" (Napoleon, 1978, p. 104).[10]

The American Experience - The Colonial Period

The men and women who first colonized the United States brought with them religious and social traditions which were clearly patriarchal in nature. For instance, most of the Protestant sects believed that Eve was the first to come under the devil's spell and that woman was responsible for all the evil in the world. Calvin and Knox, both influential in Protestant thought, were totally against equality for women, and the Colonies certainly did not escape the witch hunting fervor of the sixteenth and seventeenth centuries (Hymowitz & Weissman, 1978). However, the Puritans did believe that while the husband was to have total authority in the home, husband and wife were still expected to live with mutual affection and respect; the wife's submission was to be joyful, the husband, wise and kind. In fact, laws existed which forbade a man to beat his wife or force her to disobey God's law; she, too, was a Christian and was personally responsible to God for her actions (Altbach, 1974, p. 21).

Generally speaking, colonial women had considerable status and freedom of activity simply because their talents and labors were needed in the unsettled country. Women ran taverns, rooming houses, and acted as blacksmiths, tailors, teachers, and shopkeepers (Hymowitz & Weissman, 1978, p. 5). Women also had a reasonably good chance of owning property; land grants were sometimes given to the wives of settlers and to widows (Hymowitz & Weissman, 1978, p. 3). Because of their economic position, women also often participated in legal proceedings, such as suing to collect payments (Hymowitz & Weissman, 1978, p. 6).

Despite these advantages, however, women were definitely not the equals of men. Although laws usually applied to both men and women in cases regarding adultery and fornication, the sentences given women were ordinarily harsher than those received by men, and the punishments tended to be more humiliating and physically brutal. The dunking stool, for example, was reserved solely for women (Altbach, 1974, p. 23).

Colonial law did recognize a wife's right to share her husband's home and bed, be supported by him, and be protected from his violence (Hymowitz & Weissman, 1978, p. 23). However, women were still not permitted to sue in court, so the rights that they possessed in theory were, in practice, meaningless. It was not until the 1800's, with the growth of the women's movement, that there was any serious challenge to "couverture." Therefore, during the period of colonization, women were allowed greater flexibility in their roles only so long as these new freedoms did not substantially threaten the patriarchal system (Altbach, 1974, p. 23).

The American Revolution, while securing more rights and freedoms for men, did little to further the progress of women; there was a noticeable lack of the mention of women in both the Declaration of Independence and in the proposed Constitution. This "oversight" did not go unnoticed by all. Abigail Adams, for example, expressed her disapproval of the new power structure in a letter she wrote to her husband in April, 1776. Mr. Adams was not pleased by his wife's letter and wrote the following in reply: "At your extraordinary code of laws I cannot but laugh. We have been told that our struggle has loosened the bonds of government everywhere - children and apprentices. . .schools and colleges. . .Indians and Negroes grow insolent. But your letter was the first intimation that another tribe more numerous and powerful than the rest, were grown discontented. . . Depend on it, we know better than to repeal our masculine systems" (Adams, 1978, p. 36).

Post Revolutionary War and the Victorian Period

In the first decades of the 1800's social and economic changes took place which would have a profound effect on the lives of women for the next 170 years. In the Northeast there developed a new middle class which lived in urban areas and earned its living from business. In this middle class, home and family were seen as separate from the world of work. For the first time, women performed traditional work but earned no money for it; women were no longer seen as partners. Rather, they became dependents supported by their husbands (Hymowitz & Weissman, 1978). In addition, with the growing industrialization of the country, the factory, not the home, soon became the major producer of goods. A woman's dependency upon her husband's earnings was therefore increased, since there was no other way to obtain needed products. During this period women were also slowly closed off from a number of economic opportunities they had earlier enjoyed. For example, in many of the trades once practiced by women, formal instruction was newly required. Women were barred from this training.

With regard to legal practices in the United States, the most influential was English Common Law, which had been adopted by all the Colonies except Connecticut, and later Louisiana, which adopted the Napoleonic Code. The first United States court to acknowledge a husband's right to beat his wife was in Mississippi. In 1824, the decision in Bradley vs. the State of Mississippi found that a husband should be allowed to "moderately chastise his wife without subjecting himself to the vexatious prosecutions for assault and battery, resulting in the discredit and shame of all parties concerned" (Langley & Levy, 1978, p. 53).[11]

The next fifty or sixty years saw some improvement in statutes related to domestic violence. States such as Maryland, Alabama, and New Hampshire passed laws forbidding wifebeating (Langley & Levy, 1978, p. 54). However, a wife could still not obtain redress in court because she was a "femme couvert." And in North Carolina in 1864, a precedent was established which influenced legal decisions for well over one hundred years. In the State vs. Black, it was found that wifebeating was a matter best left out of the courts unless "some permanent injury be inflicted or there be an excess of violence. Otherwise the law will not invade the domestic forum or go behind the curtain. . ." The law was to "leave the parties to themselves as the best mode of inducing them to make the matter up and to live together as man and wife should" (Langley & Levy, 1978, pp. 53-54).[12]

During this period, there was also a great deal of discussion about what one should properly consider a man's "sphere" and a woman's "sphere." In fact, an entire theory of personality evolved based on the theory that men and women were total opposites both in physical constitutions and temperament. During the 1700's the differences between men and women were certainly acknowledged, but there was more flexibility. It was quite possible, indeed even important, for a woman during the 1700's to be strong, daring, and perhaps even adventurous. But by the 1800's, this had changed. Women soon came to be viewed as timid, gentle, helpless, and weak (Hymowitz & Weissman, 1978, p. 66).

An excellent example of this new "psychology" is found in Thomas Dew's classic dissertation "The Differences Between the Sexes:" "The greater strength of man, enables him to occupy the foreground in the picture. He leaves the domestic scenes; he plunges into the turmoil and bustle of an active, selfish world. . .hence courage and boldness are his attributes. . . He is the shield of woman, destined by nature to guard and protect her. Her inferior strength and sedentary habits confine her within the domestic circle; she is kept aloof from the bustle and storm of active life; she is not familiarized with the out of door dangers and hardships of a cold and scuffling world; timidity and modesty are her attributes. . . Grace, charm, and loveliness are the charms which constitute her power. By these she creates the magic spell that subdues to her will, the more mighty physical powers by which she is surrounded" (Dew, 1968, pp. 45-46). This emphasis on the importance of physical strength was, in truth, a spurious argument; the middle class depended on commerce. The shopkeeper, the lawyer, the doctor, and the businessman needed intellect, not physical prowess, in order to become successful. Furthermore, within only fifty years, society had conveniently chosen to forget that colonial women had routinely put in long, arduous hours both working on farms and in homes, and were therefore quite accustomed to physical labor.

Protestant theologians also expressed their views regarding the proper role for women. For example, in Jonathon Stearns' *Female Influence, and the True Christian Mode of*

Its Exercise, he stated that woman was fitted by nature to cheer the afflicted and to lighten the burden of misery, because God had endowed her with qualities which made her specially adapted for these jobs. "Much dispute has arisen in modern times with regard to the comparative intellectual ability of the sexes. . . The truth is, there is a *natural difference* in the mental as well as the physical constitution of the two classes - a difference which implies not *inferiority* on one part, but only *adaptation to a different sphere*" (Stearns, 1968, p. 48). Stearns went on to state that although there were women who were quite capable of public debate, this was not an appropriate activity. It was not a question of ability, but rather a matter of decency, and Christian propriety.

During the Victorian period, motherhood was considered the middle class woman's most important job. The bearing and raising of children became elevated to a saintly duty. It was therefore all the more important for women to retain their refinement, innocence and passivity so that they would have the proper effect on their offspring. Victorian women were also kept confined because of a prevailing belief in the inherent weakness of the female constitution. This notion was based on the law of conservation of energy, which stated that one organ or ability could not be developed without it being at the expense of all others. Since it was assumed that childbearing was the central and most important reason for a woman's existence, reproductive organs were believed to have almost total control over a woman's personality and physical health. Furthermore, it was dangerous to divert any energy away from reproduction. One of the consequences of this theory was that higher education for women was viewed by some as a potential threat to the future of the entire race. As one physician wrote, "If we wish woman to fulfill the task of motherhood fully, she cannot possess a masculine brain. If the feminine abilities were developed to the same degree as those of the male, her maternal organs would suffer and we should have before us a repulsive and useless hybrid" (Moebius, 1973, p. 28).

During the Victorian period women's lives were highly circumscribed. Medical science and psychology taught them that they were far too weak and fragile for anything but their prime duty - childbearing. Economic and legal factors kept them dependent on their husbands, and religious leaders threatened dire consequences if women dared to venture beyond their appropriate "sphere." However, the practice of keeping women at home, carefully segregated from any other activity, carried within it the seeds of its own destruction: "Ideas about women's place in the nineteenth century forced women into very close relationships with one another. When women were together, they talked about their lives. Even as they comforted one another, they also complained, and eventually they grew angry. It was no accident that the nineteenth century women's movement was conceived at a ladies' tea party" (Hymowitz & Weissman, 1978, p. 75).

The Suffrage Movement and the Emergence of the Modern Woman (1890 to the late 1960's)

By the end of the nineteenth century women had gained status in a number of areas. For example, although there had been no extensive legal reform, by 1890 many states had modified the courverture ruling, giving women control over their inherited property and earnings. Women also found new employment opportunities as typists and stenographers, for instance. However, during the 1890's the phenomenon of "feminization" occurred in many areas. "Feminization" refers to the process in which women become the majority within a profession, leaving only a very small number of men who then take the leadership positions.

The prestige of the field is thereby reduced (Banner, 1974).

Advances for women in education were less equivocal. At the beginning of the nineteenth century no colleges had accepted women. By contrast, in 1900 80% of all colleges, universities, and professional schools allowed women to enroll. The importance of these opportunities should not be underestimated; women not only increased their academic knowledge, but also gained the necessary self-confidence to eventually begin questioning their "proper" place in society (Banner, 1974, p. 6).

The 1890's also saw a growth in the number and type of women's organizations. However, the accomplishments of the suffrage movement were far from impressive. One reason for this failure was that in the late nineteenth century there was a vigorous anti-suffrage campaign, frequently led by very socially prominent women. The argument of the anti-suffrage movement was quite simple. If women voted they would eventually hold office, and if they eventually held office, they would necessarily have to leave home, thereby breaking up the families. This would also, (although it was never spoken), take power away from men. In fact, until 1912, the suffrage movement was almost nonexistent (Banner, 1974, p. 93).

In the years directly preceding 1920, however, the suffrage movement again gained strength and purpose. A new generation of leaders entered the movement, many of whom had been in England and had observed the tactics used there. In addition, the Progressives had decided to include woman's suffrage as part of their platform. Between 1910 and 1914, six states gave the vote to women. On August 18, 1920, with the passage by the State of Tennessee, the Nineteenth Amendment giving women the right to vote became law (Banner, 1974, p. 124).

With the passage of the Nineteenth Amendment, however, the women's movement seemed to lose its reason for being, and during the 1920's, the progress for women's rights in other areas was also significantly slowed. There were at least two reasons for this lack of progress. First, Freud's thought became quite influential in the United States. Freud's theory supported the pre-existing gynecological view that the female personality was inherently defective. The true cause for this deficiency, however, was not the presence of a dominating uterus, but rather the lack of a penis. According to Freud, men developed social virtues because their superegos were strengthened by overcoming the Oedipal complex. The primary factor in this process was the fear of castration. Since women lacked this fear, they never completely freed themselves from this complex, and were therefore prone to envy and jealousy and had a weaker capacity for sublimation. According to Freud, all girsl also suffered from penis envy, which could result in personality disturbances. "Here what has been named the masculinity complex in women branches off. It may put great difficulties in the way of the regular development towards femininity, if it cannot be got over soon enough. The hope of someday obtaining a penis, in spite of everything, and so becoming like a man, may persist to an incredibly late age and may become a motive for strange and otherwise unaccountable actions. . . Thus a girl may refuse to accept the fact of being castrated, may harden herself in the conviction that she does possess a penis, and may subsequently be compelled to behave as though she were a man" (Freud, 1961, p. 253).

In the same article Freud also made it clear that anatomical differences resulted in differences in personality. "I cannot evade the notion. . .that for women the level of what is ethically normal is different from what it is in men. Their superego is never so inexorable, so impersonal, so independent of its emotional origin as we require it to be in men.

Character traits which critics of every epoch have brought up against women - that they show less sense of justice than men, that they are less ready to submit to the great exigencies of life, that they are more often influenced in their judgments by feelings of affection or hostility - all of these would be amply accounted for by the modification in the formation of their superego which we have inferred above. We must not allow ourselves to be deflected from such conclusions by the denials of feminists, who are anxious to force us to regard the two sexes as completely equal in position and worth. . ." (Freud, 1961, pp. 257-258). Freud's psychology lent more "scientific support" to the belief that women should be confined to domestic activities.

Second, Americans seemed to be somewhat tired of reform causes. By the mid-1920's the consensus was that women had indeed attained total liberation because suffrage had been won. This belief led to a backlash, and by the late 1920's, there was a new anti-feminism arguing that women simply weren't capable of successfully combining a marriage and a career (O'Neill, 1969, p. 315). Women were supposed to be homemakers, and those activities were glamorized and pictured as self-fulfilling (Banner, 1974, p. 143). Feminists and anti-feminists alike seemed to be agreed that women had unique qualities, and as a sex demanded very special treatment. "With God, Freud, Marx, nature, and a host of lesser authorities apparently agreed that woman's unique character was sexual and her destiny maternal, ambitious women eager to play out the old drama of emancipation had little working for them" (O'Neill, 1969, p. 316). The women who did work often became disillusioned as they found that "juggling" career and family in a society not totally supportive of those efforts was a very difficult task. ". . .the mass of educated married women no longer believed that paid employment was worth the trouble. Why should they exhaust themselves with complicated alternatives to their usual routines when it was easier to stay at home and cultivate that higher domesticity which, it was now understood, had been the real purpose of the women's movement all along?" (O'Neill, 1969, p. 332)

The Depression and Second World War served to reinforce the view that a woman's proper role was as a wife and mother; economic and political problems and uncertainties made a stable, traditional family life seem very desirable. During the war, of course, women had worked in large numbers, and had been praised for their participation and sacrifice for the national good. However, the woman who worked in the post-war years was no longer being patriotic - she was taking a much-needed job away from a returning veteran.

Not surprisingly, a return to domesticity was publically advocated, supported by the psychological thought of the time. For instance, during the 1940's, Freud's work became popularized by writers such as Helen Deutsch. In her highly influential work, *The Psychology of Women*, she stated that any woman who viewed herself as being other than passive was, quite simply, suffering from a masculinity complex. Deutsch's description of women as feminine/passive and men as masculine/active was reminiscent of the nineteenth century controversy over the proper spheres for men and women. In fact, the most extreme Freudians did recommend a return to traditionalism, a position defined in the popular book, *Modern Woman - The Lost Sex*. Written by a psychiatrist and sociologist, the book attacked the cultural devaluation of homemaking and motherhood, and claimed that women's desires for "masculine" activities and achievements were responsible for the high level of neurosis and dissatisfaction in society. The solution to this problem was the "feminine mother," the only woman who could raise healthy children. "How does the proper mother bring up her children? . . .she accepts her sexuality and enjoys it without parading it. She does not understand when she hears other women speak bitterly of the privileges of men. She does not see things that way. Men, to her, are useful objects and if, being useful, they extract enjoyment from various of the strange things they are up to it is quite all right with her. She knows, at any rate, that she is dependent on a man. There is no fantasy in her mind about being an 'independent woman,' a contradiction in terms. . . Having children is to her the most natural thing possible. . . When she hears someone question the advisability of having children she is bewildered unless she is told of some trenchant medical reason. Then she feels sorry for the woman deprived. If a woman does not have children, she asks ingenuously, what is everything all about for her?" (Lundberg & Farnham, 1947, p. 319).

The problems of women in the 1940's, '50's, and early '60's were eloquently summed up and given voice in the now classic, *The Feminine Mystique* by Betty Friedan. In it she described quite cogently the image of the ideal woman. "The American housewife - freed by science and labor saving appliances from drudgery, the dangers of childbirth, and the illnesses of her grandmother. She was healthy, beautiful, educated, and concerned only about her husband, her children, and her home. She had found true feminine fulfillment. As a housewife and mother, she was respected as a full and equal partner to man in his world. She was free to choose automobiles, clothes, appliances, supermarkets; she had everything that women ever dreamed of" (Friedan, 1974, p. 13). The image-makers of that era, primarily the popular magazines, geared their material for the woman who fit the above description. For instance, an editor of a large woman's magazine at the time described his readers as being concerned only about the family and home. Women were not interested in travel, politics, public issues, national, or international affairs. They didn't understand satire, abstract ideas, or current issues. Furthermore, while it was at least acceptable for the "ideal" woman of the 1950's to work outside the home, a more traditional role was clearly preferable. For example, in 1956 the October 16th issue of *Look* stated, "The American woman is winning the battle of the sexes. Like a teenager, she is growing up and confounding her critics. . . No longer a psychological immigrant to man's world, she works, rather casually, as a third of the U.S. labor force, less towards a "big career" than as a way of filling a hope chest or buying a new home freezer. She gracefully concedes the top jobs to men. This wondrous creature also marries younger than ever, has more babies and looks and acts far more feminine than the "emancipated girl" of the 1920's and 1930's. Steel worker's wife and junior leaguer alike do their own housework. . . Today if she makes an old fashioned choice, and lovingly tends a garden and a bumper crop of children, she rates louder hosannahs than ever before" (Look Magazine, 1974, pp. 52-53).[13]

But if American society were loud in praise of the "traditional woman," it had scorn and criticism for the woman who dared venture outside of that role. The bright, well educated, and ambitious career woman was described as being frustrated and so masculinzed by her career that her husband became indifferent to her sexually and usually drowned his problems and his destroyed masculinity in alcoholism. But it wasn't enough to be the housewife and model mother in terms of behavior alone. It was clear that the ideal woman's whole psychological, emotional and spiritual life was to be immersed in those activities. For example, the Christmas, 1956 issue of Life magazine warned of the dangers of the woman who had either worked before marriage or was well educated and then found herself discontented with being "just a housewife." This dissatisfaction could work "as much damage on the lives of her husband and children (and her own life) as if she were a career woman, and indeed sometimes more" (Life Magazine, 1974, p. 52).

CHAPTER II

CONDITIONS CURRENTLY CONTRIBUTING TO THE INCIDENCE OF WIFE ABUSE

Because of the vigor and scope of the women's movement in the last few years, one might conclude that factors which once existed to support the institution of wifebeating are no longer present. However, it has been estimated that there is some level of violence in from fifty to sixty percent of American homes (Straus, 1978, p. 447). Obviously, there are still factors which perpetuate the physical abuse of women. First, there is empirical evidence that conjugal violence is still informally sanctioned. For example, one attitude survey found that one fifth of all Americans approved of slapping one's spouse on "appropriate occasions." Furthermore, the higher the respondent's education and income level, the more likely he or she was to approve of physical aggression between husband and wife (McEvoy & Stark, 1970, p. 52). In addition, in a recent laboratory study, subjects were given identical descriptions of an assault by a man on a woman. Half of the participants were told that the victim and assailant were strangers, the other half, that they were married. The punishment recommended for the man was far less severe when it was believed that the couple were husband and wife (Churchill & Straus, Note 1). Finally, in a field study, assaults were staged on a streetcorner. Male witnesses came to the aid of men being assaulted by other men, helped women being assaulted by other women, and even interceded for men being attacked by women. However, not one male bystander intervened to help when a woman was assaulted by a man (Borofsky, Stollak & Messe, 1971). Therefore, a large number of Americans apparently approve of violence and use it in marital relationships.

It also appears that depicting the physical abuse of women is lucrative; record album covers, billboards, and advertisements picture women bound, gagged, whipped, chained, and as victims of murder, sexual assault, and gang rape: ". . .pornographic material portraying rape, torture, murder, bondage, and sado-machochistic perversions for erotic stimulation and pleasure has literally flooded the market" (London, 1978, p. 510). However degrading, these images apparently sell well. For example, the Atlantic/Avco Records magazine copy of The Rolling Stones' album, "Black and Blue" pictures a woman who has obviously been beaten. Although this woman is still tied up, she appears seductive, as if asking for more abuse. In truth, of course, a bruised and battered woman's face is hardly appealing. However, the photo gives the impression that no real damage has been done. Both billboard and the magazine article stated, "I'm black and blue from The Rolling Stones, and I love it." This graphic was used in at least five major industry consumer magazines for a period of two months.

Images such as these are not necessarily designed to reach men. For instance, in 1976, *Vogue* magazine featured a twelve page "spread" showing a man first caressing and then menacing the female model. The dramatic peak of the sequence occurred when the man smashed the woman across the face. In addition, the woman actually appears to have enjoyed the treatment, since on the next page she is shown touching him affectionately. Images like these clearly distort the reality of violence against women, thereby contributing to its incidence and maintenance (London, 1978, p. 519).

Domestic violence is also perpetuated by the fact that current myths and stereotypes about wife abuse tend to make the victim feel ashamed and reluctant to seek help, and also cause others to view her as undeserving of aid. To begin with, many people believe that the battered woman stays "because she likes it" (Walton[14], Note 2; Leech[15], Note 3). This myth has two implications, both of which are false. First, it suggests that battered women are masochists who are sexually aroused by physical abuse. While this may be a popular notion, it does not have basis in fact; research has shown that few, if any, victims are masochists (Gayford, 1975). As one experienced counselor put it, "I have yet to see a woman who got sexual pleasure from having her nose broken and her eyes blackened" (Leech, Note 4). The effect of this belief is that people often see little reason to help a person who purposefully chooses to be mistreated. Furthermore, the battered woman herself may also come to believe the myth. Regardless of how she really feels, she may begin to suspect that perhaps she really is a masochist. This usually increases her shame, and makes it less likely that she will tell anyone about the problem (Walton, Note 5).

The second implication is that getting out of a violent situation is easy; the woman is an adult, "the door is open," so she need only take her children and go. However, the battered woman often has economic difficulties. For example, she may not have a job or job skills. Confronted with the prospect of having to support herself and her children, she may decide that beatings are the price she must pay for financial security. Even when women are employed, they often discover that it is difficult to find landlords who will rent to single women with children (Hofeller[16]; Leech, Note 6).

It is also widely - and incorrectly, believed that men almost always have good reason for attacking their wives. It is not uncommon for friends, relatives, or police to ask a battered woman, "What did you do to provoke him?" (Hofeller; Leech, Note 7; Walton, Note 8). Such an attitude not only provides the man with justification for his violence, but can also discourage a woman from leaving; if she is convinced that abuse is truly her fault, it is her responsibility to behave in such a manner that it doesn't happen again (Walton, Note 9).

Current economic conditions may also influence the battered woman to stay with her husband; it is often difficult for women to support themselves since they are still primarily concentrated in a small number of low paying occupations, with relatively few being found in professional and technical fields. Furthermore, in one study of income levels, a national probability sample was used, and occupational prestige, length of employment and number of hours worked were controlled. Even with these factors removed, a woman still made an average of $3458.00 less than a man in a comparable position. By 1973, this figure had improved by only 1% (Larwood & Wood, 1977, p. 12).

There is also evidence that women who are divorced experience economic deprivation. For example, in 1969, the median income of families with children headed by women age 25 to 44 was $4000.00 a year. By contrast, the two parent home median was $11,600.00. In addition, only 9% of female headed families of all races had incomes over $10,000, while 55% of two parent homes did. In short, a large number of women may expect to suffer downward mobility following divorce. Finally, women cannot always depend on alimony; the majority of men do not contribute to their wives' and children's support after the separation (Brandwein, Brown & Fox, 1974, p. 500).

With regard to legal aspects, it is true that some progress has been made; no law presently exists giving men the right to abuse their wives. However, only eleven states have specific statutes which deal with domestic violence, and in only one state - California - is wifebeating a felony offense (Flemming, Note 10). Furthermore, even in California, for example, where a woman is theoretically protected from the violence of her husband, it is, in practice, still very difficult to obtain redress, and a woman who wishes to take legal action faces an enormous and discouraging task. First, although wifebeating is defined as a felony, it is at the responding officer's discretion to decide whether or not a beating is a felony or a misdemeanor. If the officer decides that the assault was a misdemeanor, he cannot make an arrest unless he actually saw the beating in progress. If a woman wants her husband arrested, she herself must make a citizen's arrest. Most women do not have the courage or fortitude to do this - and with good reason. Even if a woman signs a complaint against her spouse and has him arrested, he is still eligible to post bail and can be back out on the streets or in the house to beat her up again within two or three hours (Bustus[17], Note 11). Many women have received severe beatings from their recently released husbands (Hofeller).

The woman who has the determination to actually press criminal charges against her husband faces many obstacles. For example, district attorneys are naturally reluctant to take cases without sufficient evidence, and evidence is often very difficult to get in domestic violence cases. Beatings are often unwitnessed crimes. Even when there have been witnesses, they are usually reluctant to become involved. The best evidence, of course, is the actual physical harm done to the woman. However, the trial is usually not held for six or eight months, when bruises have healed. If a woman does not have a doctor's report or pictures of her injuries, it is unlikely that a jury will necessarily take her word over that of her husband (Bustus, Note 12). Furthermore, the very act of obtaining evidence, that is of having one's nude body photographed at a police station, is a traumatic experience, and a woman who has just been beaten is already in trauma. In addition, a woman who wants to press charges must find a safe place for herself and her children to stay while awaiting trial. For the woman with limited financial means, this is often impossible. Faced with the prospect of living with the man she is taking to court, and coping with the resulting fear and threat of further injury, it is not surprising that many women drop charges.

A woman may also be deterred by other factors. For example, she may begin to feel sorry for her husband and not want him to lose his job, have a record, or go to jail. The unemployed husband also presents a very real threat to a woman who is dependent upon her spouse for support. Even if a woman does go to court, the action itself can be humiliating. During a trial any aspects of the woman's life are considered "fair game," and, as in the case of rape, the defense makes every effort to show that the woman indeed provoked her husband to violence. Without the emotional support of someone close to her, either family, friend, or advocate, the whole process of the many court appearances and the strain of trial is one which discourages the majority of women (Bustus, Note 13).

Although criminal prosecution is very difficult, under the right circumstances many women do press charges and follow through. For example, in an innovative project in Louisville, Kentucky, women advocates appear with plaintiffs in court and provide them with constant emotional support. At present, only 13% of the women who begin criminal proceedings with this program ever dropped charges (Calzaretta, Note 14).

Civil proceedings are often as frustrating and as discouraging. At present, a restraining order is the only civil action a woman can take, and it affords her no physical protection. Violation of a "Temporary Restraining Order, Domestic Relations" is not a misdemeanor; the respondent is merely in contempt of court. Furthermore, even with the new restraining order 527b, where violation is a misdemeanor, the officer must still see the husband in the act of violating the order. Unfortunately, many women with restraining orders are seen by the police after the spouse has already come and beaten them. In short, although existing laws protect a woman from violence in her own home, in practice the only real recourse she has is to either buy herself protection or to move herself and her children to safer surroundings.

Religious views regarding domestic violence have also changed in theory; it would be rare if not unheard of to have a pastor or priest advocate a husband's use of physical force against his wife. In practice, however, some of the fundamentalist denominations and the Catholic Church, which view divorce as unacceptable and adhere to traditional roles, make it very difficult for a woman to end a relationship in which there is violence. Although some younger priests and pastors are aware of the problem of wifebeating and can offer counsel and support to a battered woman, it would appear that a majority of clerics are either unaware or unwilling to become involved. For example, in June, 1979, House of Ruth [18] presented a workshop on domestic violence. Information was sent to eighty local churches. One pastor attended. Furthermore, this level of response is not atypical (Friedman[19], Note 15; Leech, Note 16). In August, 1979, House of Ruth sent a handbook on domestic violence to each of 120 churches in the area, with information on how to obtain more free copies. One request for extra handbooks was received. Finally, counselors on hotlines have been faced with a situation many times of talking to women who were told by priests and friends that the "Christian" thing to do would be to forgive her husband. A number of women have called a local hot line asking for reassurance that they are not committing a major sin by dissolving a marriage in which the woman and sometimes the children were brutally beaten (Hofeller).

It cannot be denied that the activities of women's liberation have substantially altered and made more flexible the traditional masculine and feminine roles. However, although many men and women may be trying new ways of relating to one another, it is important to note that the traditional model of proper behavior still exists, and even thrives. For example, only a few years ago a popular book, *How to Get and Hold a Woman*, written by a marriage counselor, gave men the following advice: "Why ask women when they only need to be told? Why ask women when they hope to be taken? . . .feelings, moods, and attitudes rule a woman, not facts, reason, or logic. . . The acquisition of knowledge or responsibility does not lessen women's need for support, guidance, and control. Quite the contrary" (Payetter, 1971, p. 53). In addition, during the late 1960's an article called "The Power of Sexual Surrender" appeared in many women's magazines, and described the "masculine" woman as clear thinking and successful in business, but also frigid, driving, and competitive. If she were to be really healthy, she would have to surrender to her true nature, that is, devote herself to children and home. Only then would she come into her full power. It is important to note that this destiny is a biological one much like that touted a hundred years ago. Still another myth presented in this article was that a woman's first and foremost role in life was to be nurturant and supportive. "Women must give and give and give again because it is their one and only way to obtain happiness for themselves. . ." (Stern, 1971, p. 55[20]).

But today's woman need not merely content herself by reading about the role she should fulfill. There are now classes she can take to learn how to be a woman. She can be a "total" woman, or a "fascinating" woman, depending upon preference and pocketbook. The advice given to the prospective "total" woman at least starts out as egalitarian; women are told that they must understand, accept, and love, and above all, be themselves. In addition, sex is seen as a very positive force in marriage, and women are encouraged to learn about their own responses and fully participate in the act. However, the cornerstone of the "total" woman philosophy is that a woman must adapt herself to her husband at all times. "It is only when a woman surrenders her life to her husband, reveres and worships him, and is willing to serve him, that she becomes really beautiful to him. She becomes a priceless jewel, the glory of feminity, his queen" (Morgan, 1973, pp. 96-97).

To be a "fascinating" woman, one must also give up any sense of self-determination. Women are told that in order to be proper wives and mothers they must eliminate any masculine capabilities they have. They are to be frail, dependent, submissive, and like a little girl. Women should not work unless the family is on the brink of total poverty, because their earning power would be a threat to the man and his masculine role. If it is absolutely necessary that she work, then she must stay in "feminine" jobs such as teaching or nursing. Even so, dividing her time between two worlds, it is hard for a woman to succeed in either. At all costs, a woman must never compete with a man. "A competent woman stands as a threat to the male ego - to his position and capabilities as a man" (Andelin, 1974, p. 153). Furthermore, women are supposed to enjoy this role because it is their nature. Women must freely and happily give themselves to husband and family because, "Remember, *a woman's glory is the success of her husband, the happiness of her children, and her overall success in the home*" [emphasis Andelin's] (Andelin, 1974, p. 237).

The final authority for the delineation of masculine and feminine roles in both these philosophies rests with God and the Bible, just as it did one hundred years ago. And lest one think that the "total" woman and the "fascinating" woman are just the "fringe," it should be remembered that thousands of women have taken these classes. There is still considerable cultural support of a very traditional feminine role.

It is also necessary to consider the current societal stereotype of masculinity. With regard to socialization, for example, one study found that demands made on boys were more stringent than those made on girls, were made at an earlier age, and were frequently enforced more harshly (Hartley, 1959). More recent research (Maccoby & Jacklin, 1974) has confirmed that the socialization of boys is more intense; they receive more pressure against behaving in a sex-inappropriate manner, are more frequently punished, and also tend to be praised and encouraged more than girls. There is also evidence from group studies that boys make more attempts to dominate one another than do girls (Maccoby & Jacklin, 1974).

The pressure to avoid anything feminine can result in "compulsive masculinity." As Hartley has pointed out, "When he [a boy] sees women as weak, easily damaged, lacking strength in mind and body, able to perform only tasks which take the least strength and are of least importance, what boy in his right senses would not give his all to escape this alternative to the male role? For many, unfortunately, the scramble to escape takes on all the aspects of panic, and the outward semblance of non-feminity is achieved at a tremendous cost of anxiety and self-alienation" (Hartley,

1959, p. 12).

Adherence to a rigid masculine role can be both physically and psychologically damaging. First, men are expected to achieve, get ahead, and stay "cool." However, winning once is not enough; to be a "real" man, one has to keep winning. Not surprisingly, the need to stay ahead produces considerable stress (Vleck & Sawyer, 1974). Furthermore, it has been suggested that this tension may be partially responsible for the fact that men have a higher risk of heart attack and tend to die earlier than women (Jouard, 1974). Second, men also tend to be low in self-disclosure, which frequently interferes with the establishment of interpersonal relationships; the man who is afraid to reveal himself is likely to view potential intimacy as threatening (Jouard, 1974). Third, men are taught that ". . .'real men' are never passive or dependent, always dominant in relationships with women or other men, and don't talk about or directly express feelings; especially feelings that don't contribute to dominance" (Fasteau, 1972, p. 19). Finally, men are generally trained not to notice both physical and emotional feelings until they become so strong that it is no longer possible to ignore them. It is quite possible that batterers are unaware of frustration or anger, until the pressures are unbearable. These men then overreact with physical aggression. The violence would not only allow for an acceptable "male" display of emotion, but also re-establish the man in his "proper" dominant position.

Rigid definitions of masculine and feminine also exist among some professionals; a number of psychiatrists and psy chologists still apparently advocate a very restrictive and biologically determined role for women. For example, consider Joseph Rheingold's statement that, ". . .woman is nurturance . . .anatomy decrees the life of a woman. . .when women grow up without dread of their biological functions and without subversion by feminist doctrines and therefore enter upon motherhood with a sense of fulfillment and altruistic sentiment we shall attain the goal of a good life and a secure world in which to live" (Rheingold, 1971, p. 754). This might just as well have been written one hundred years ago.

Another belief which still enjoys some support is that women are by nature masochistic. The practitioner who adheres to this theory tends to make judgments about the battered woman which can interfere with effective treatment. The "traditional" explanation for wife abuse is that women seek out relationships with assaultive men due to the inherent masochistic tendencies in all women; wives stay in the relationship simply because it gives them satisfaction to suffer (Symonds, 1979). According to Symonds, all psychiatrists have been influenced to some degree by that concept. As she stated,

> "While I personally stopped accepting Freud's theory of feminine psychology from the time I read Karen Horney in 1945, I had a different explanation in which interpersonal dynamics and interacting personality patterns explained it for me. This was that the dependent personality interacts with the aggressive, arrogant, vindictive personality in a mutually satisfying way. While in general this is true. . .my theoretical explanations merely served me as a convenient way to push aside an unpleasant and painful condition. What we all tried to push aside was an honest confrontation with the situation, one which would have caused us anxiety, and one which would have threatened us in another manner. What we did not recognize is that we were responding in a stereotypic way to victims of crime. It is now known that we all have an unconscious need to reject the victim" (Symonds, 1979, p. 162).

Psychologists and psychiatrists have also been hampered by the fact that until recently very few women ever sought help because of violence in their relationships. Therefore, the helping professions tend to lack adequate and effective techniques for dealing with the complex problem of domestic violence. Counselors often report that they feel inadequate in dealing with spouse abuse because they not only lack knowledge of the dynamics involved, but are also unaware of the legal alternatives available to their clients (Hofeller; Walton, Note 17). Therefore, there are still economic, religious, legal, and cultural factors which contribute to the current level of domestic violence.

CHAPTER III

EMPIRICAL RESEARCH ON DOMESTIC VIOLENCE

Although wifebeating is by no means a new phenomenon, it is only in the last ten years that social scientists have begun to study the problem. Therefore, the amount of empirical data available is relatively small. Nevertheless, it is possible to identify some of the variables in domestic violence and classify them as either (1) factors associated with the individuals involved, (e.g. role perceptions and personality traits); (2) social factors, (e.g. family background); or (3) situational factors, (e.g. stresses due to unemployment.

Personality Factors

One of the most salient characteristics of most wifebeaters is their strict adherence to a rigidly defined male role. This compulsive masculinity, or "machismo" as it is popularly called, is reflected in an attempt to maintain total dominance over their wives (Davidson, 1978; Martin, 1976; Walker, 1979). The majority of abusive men are also extremely jealous and possessive of their mates (Hilberman, 1978; Scott, 1974; Walker, 1979). Sometimes this jealousy becomes pathological. For example, one husband was so suspicious of his wife that when she wanted to use the ladies' room at a public facility, he personally escorted her to the door (Walker, 1979, p. 38). Although most of this jealousy has a sexual basis, some men also appear to resent the time wives spend caring for children, for example (Martin, 1977).

Despite their desire to fulfill a traditional masculine role, many batterers also have elements of helplessness and dependency in their personalities (Davidson, 1978; Hilberman & Munson, 1978; Martin, 1976). The violent husband has been described as a ". . .little boy, wanting to be grown up and superior, as he'd been taught he should be, yet was not in fact; requiring those around him to join in his pretense if he were to survive emotionally, and his family survive physically" (Davidson, 1978, p. 29). Therefore, when an abusive man perceives a threat to his ego or masculine prerogative, he responds with the only acceptable emotional outburst for males - anger and aggression.

It has also been suggested that wifebeaters may be described as either "treatable" or "intractable," depending upon whether or not they view their violence as a legitimate behavior. For the "intractable" batterer, violence is a normal part of his lifestyle; he sees nothing wrong with abusing his wife. By contrast, the "treatable" husband experiences extreme guilt and remorse after an incident. This type of man ordinarily attempts to maintain tight control over all his emotions. When this control does break down, he reacts with approved masculine aggression rather than a "feminine" response such as become hysterical or having a nervous breakdown. If the "treatable" husband can be convinced to seek counseling, it may be possible for him to learn non-violent methods of coping (Davidson, 1978, p. 23).

The fact that assaultive men tend to lack verbal communication skills (Davidson, 1978; Gelles, 1972; Prescott & Letko, 1977) may also be a precipitating factor in violent episodes; a number of women have reported that beatings were sometimes preceded by a verbal argument in which neither partner communicated effectively. The question was settled by the husband who simply used physical force to end the discussion (Davidson, 1978; Gelles, 1972; Martin, 1976). However, their inability to communicate verbally does not necessarily mean that all batterers are withdrawn, or seek to avoid interaction with people. On the contrary, many men who abuse their wives can be very friendly, warm, and charming with selected others (Davidson, 1978; Walter, 1979). The contrast between public and private behavior is sometimes so distinct that women report that their husbands seem to have two different personalities (Walker, 1979). Finally, wives often describe their abusive husbands as insecure, moody, angry, and resentful (Martin, 1976). "The battering husband is likely to be a 'loser' in some basic way. He is probably angry with himself and frustrated by his life. He may put up a good front in public, but in the privacy and intimacy of his home he may not be able to hide, either from himself or his wife, his feelings of inadequacy and low self-esteem. The man who is losing his grip on his job or his prospects may feel compelled to prove that he is at least the master of his home. Beating his wife is one way for him to appear a winner" (Martin, 1976, p. 45). Therefore, there is evidence to suggest that many assaultive men may become violent because of their inability to fulfill a traditional, dominant, male role.

Many battered women tend to hold stereotyped attitudes regarding appropriate masculine and feminine behavior. As Davidson (1978) has pointed out, "'. . .The victims may exemplify society's old image of ideal womanhood - submissive, religious, nonassertive, accepting of whatever the husband's life brings. . . The husband comes first for these women, who perceive themselves as having little control over many areas of their own lives" (Davidson, 1978, p. 51). Furthermore, the battered woman often views men as superior, and all women, including herself, as inferior (Davidson, 1978). Therefore, it is not surprising that both researchers and counselors report that almost all abused wives have very low self-esteem (Carlson, 1977; Roy, 1978; Walker, 1979).

In contrast to their husbands, battered women have a tendency to cope with anger by either denying it, or by turning it inward, resulting in depression, psychosomatic illnesses and feelings of guilt (Hilberman & Munson, 1978; Walker, 1979). Of course, not all abused wives are totally meek and submissive; some women report having engaged in pitched verbal arguments with their spouses, even resorting to violence themselves at times (Gelles, 1972).

Although it does appear that certain personality factors are associated with wifebeating, there are two reasons that these findings should be interpreted with caution. First, data in the above-mentioned sources were primarily anecdotal; no study cited described how the information had been obtained (i.e. whether or not a specific instrument had been used in personality assessment). Second, personality factors cannot be viewed as causal; information about individual traits and role perceptions was obtained after or during the experience with abuse, never before the violence began.

Social Factors

It is not yet possible to identify one set of demographics which can reliably differentiate between violent and nonviolent couples (Carlson, 1977; Davidson, 1978; Martin, 1976; Roy, 1977; Walker, 1979). Unless samples are specifically drawn from certain populations, such as in Hilberman and Munson's study (1978), which used only low-income families, wifebeating does not appear to be confined to any particular socio-economic level, age group, occupation or religion.

Although childhood experiences of the man and woman may be a factor in wife abuse, the influence of such experiences has not been completely determined. For example, in some samples approximately one half of the batterers had been exposed to some form of violence (wife abuse or child abuse) in their families of origin (Carlson, 1977, p. 456; Gayford, 1975, p. 241). The highest percentage of husbands from violent homes was 81.1% (Roy, 1977, p. 30). The percentage of abused women from violent backgrounds is generally less (Walker, 1979). For example, Gayford (1975, p. 240) found that only 23 out of 100 women had had models of violence in childhood, and in Carlson's research (1977, p. 456) one third of the victims grew up in families in which wife abuse had occurred. However, one study did find that women whose mothers had been beaten were significantly more likely to become battered wives themselves than were women from non-violent backgrounds. However, there was no relationship between a woman's being abused as a child and her later mistreatment by her husband (Parker & Schumacher, 1977, p. 761). Therefore, until more research is conducted, no definitive conclusions can be drawn regarding the relative importance of childhood exposure to domestic violence.

Although no quantitative results were presented, Walker (1979) did report that the assaultive man tended to have had an abnormal relationships with his mother while growing up, and later felt considerable ambivalence toward her. In addition, in one study of husbands who had attempted to murder their wives, it was found that the subjects had been quite dependent on their mothers and had subsequently transferred these dependency needs to their wives. Whenever these men perceived a threatened withdrawal of love, they tended to react with violence (Martin, 1976).

Situational Variables

There is considerable evidence to indicate that situational stresses effect the level of spousal violence. For instance, unemployment, job dissatisfaction, and financial difficulties are frequently associated with episodes of battering (Gelles, 1972; Prescott & Letko, 1977; Roy, 1977). Other pressures, such as unexpected expenses or an unwanted pregnancy may also precipitate a beating (Gelles, 1972; Prescott & Letko, 1977; Roy, 1977). Status inequality may also represent a source of frustration. For example, in one sample of middle-class families (N=150) violence tended to occur more often when the wife was earning more money than her spouse or had attained a higher educational level than he (O'Brien, 1969).

Chronic and acute alcohol abuse is also frequently correlated with incidents of abuse (Gayford, 1975; Gelles, 1972; Hilberman & Munson, 1978; Martin, 1976; Walker, 1979). In addition, there appears to be a tendency for violence to be more severe in cases where the husband is a consistent drinker (Walker, 1979). However, the relationship between alcohol use and violence is not invariable; beatings can also occur when men are sober (Davidson, 1978; Martin, 1976), and there have been instances when batterers have managed to stop drinking, yet continued to abuse their wives (Walker, 1979). Furthermore, most authorities agree that alcohol is not a direct causal agent. Instead, drunkeness provides a socially acceptable explanation for the violence, since individuals are allowed to disavow their behavior while under the influence of alcohol. Therefore, the husband has a ready-made excuse, and the wife can "save face" by blaming the liquor, not her husband or herself, for the abuse (Gelles, 1972; Martin, 1976; Walker, 1979).

Theories of Domestic Violence

The Social Structural Theory. According to Gelles (1972), violence is a direct response to certain structural and situational stimuli. In order for violence to occur, two preconditions must be met. First, there must be either structural or situational stress. Second, the potential batterer must have been socialized to view violence as an appropriate response to certain situations, such as instances when he feels frustrated or angry. Furthermore, it is assumed that families with less education, lower occupational status, and lower income are more likely to encounter both structural and situational stress. Finally, it is assumed that individuals in different socio-economic groups are differentially socialized with regard to the acceptability of violence. Based on the above premises, Gelles concludes that violence is more likely to occur in families of lower socio-economic levels.

Although both stress and exposure to violence in family background are often associated with wife abuse, Gelles' theory is inadequate for several reasons. First, it fails to account for the fact that wife abuse can also occur even when the husband did not experience any violence in his family of origin (Carlson, 1977; Gayford, 1975). Second, there is not enough evidence to support the conclusion that violence is necessarily more prevalent among lower classes. For example, a comparison of the number of wife abuse calls received from a Harlem precinct and from Norwalk, Connecticut (a city with wide socio-economic range) revealed that both areas produced approximately the same number of wife abuse complaints (Barden, 1974, p. 38). In addition, there are at least three reasons that wife abuse in both middle and upper classes is seriously under-reported. First, the woman from a higher socio-economic level simply has more resources at her disposal for coping with the problem. For example, instead of getting treatment at a hospital emergency room, she can visit her private physician. Insteal of calling the police, she might have the money to get away for a few days. Second, many middle and upper class women report feeling extreme shame and embarrassment because of the belief that abuse occurred only in the lower classes. For many women, humiliation was a primary factor in keeping them from reporting the crime to police (Hofeller; Walton, Note 18). Finally, men in the upper and middle class necessarily have jobs with more prestige, and may even hold positions of responsibility in the community. Many of their wives feel a strong obligation to protect their husbands from any public damage or perhaps even ruin a career (Hofeller; Walton, Note 19). Therefore, although Gelles' theory can account for some violence, it is not an adequate explanation of the incidence of wife abuse.

Cycle Theory of Violence. Although Walker's "cycle theory" (1979) does not deal directly with the causes of wifebeating, it does attempt to explain why the battered woman stays in a violent situation. Walker has described domestic violence as a pattern consisting of three separate cycles. In the first phase, the tension building stage, a number of minor battering incidents occur. The wife usually copes with these episodes by denying her own anger or by deciding that she has done something to deserve the abuse. Battered women also tend to minimize the importance and/or severity of such beatings. Walker points out that this attempt on the part of the woman to "smooth over" the situation may be perceived by the man as acceptance of his abusive behavior. Therefore, he makes no subsequent effort to control himself. Coping techniques used by both husband and wife become less effective as each one senses an escalation of tension. Towards the end of this phase, minor battering incidents become more frequent. Finally, stress between the two becomes "unbearable," and stage two begins.

Phase two contains the tensions that were built up during the first phase, which are uncontrollably discharged in an acute battering incident of considerable severity. The violence in this stage is unpredictable and characterized by a rage that is so great that, according to Walker, ". . .it (the anger) blinds his control over his behavior. He starts out wanting to teach the woman a lesson . . .and stops when he feels she has learned her lesson. By this time, however, she has generally been very severely beaten" (Walker, 1979, p. 60). The second phase of the cycle is briefer than the first, usually lasting from two to twenty-four hours. According to Walker, most acute cases of violence occur when there are no witnesses. When the attack is over, it is usually followed by shock, denial, and disbelief, oftentimes on the part of the woman, and sometimes on the part of the man as well.

The woman's victimization becomes complete in phase three, where there is an unusual period of calm. The batterer behaves in a consistently charming and loving manner. He is sorry for what he has done, begs for forgiveness, and promises he will never do it again. This loving behavior is essentially the woman's reinforcement for staying in the relationship. The exact length of phase three has not been determined; sometimes it seems to last no more than a moment. Furthermore, it is rarely possible to specify exactly the point at which this phase is over. However, sooner or later, phase one tension building occurs again and a new cycle begins.

Although the concept of learned helplessness is not central to her cycle theory, Walker does discuss this phenomenon in detail, offering it as a major factor in the maintenance of physical abuse. The theory of learned helplessness in humans is based on Seligman's research with dogs.[21] Seligman administered electrical shocks at random to dogs who were in cages and could not excape. These animals learned very fast that, regardless of the response they made, there was no way that they could control the shocks. Eventually, the dogs ceased all voluntary activity; they became compliant, passive, and submissive. When the researchers tried to change this behavior, by teaching the dogs how to escape, the animals would not respond. In fact, it took repeated dragging of the dogs to the exit to teach them to act voluntarily once again.

Walker feels that, like a dog in Seligman's study, the battered woman may quickly learn that nothing she does changes her husband's behavior. Furthermore, her attempts to get the police, family, or friends to intervene and successfully end the beatings may fail. Therefore, the woman eventually decides that she has no control over her life, and becomes depressed, anxious, and submissive.

Even though the battered wife syndrome appears to contain elements of learned helplessness, such as depression and passiveness in the women, Walker's theory cannot account for the fact that many women do leave violent husbands without ever having had a chance to "practice" necessary behaviors such as initiating legal proceedings, organizing finances, and finding a safe place to stay. No one "drags them over to the other side," so to speak, as was done with the experimental animals. Many women do successfully make new responses to the violent situation - they leave.

CHAPTER IV

PRESENTATION OF THE CURRENT STUDY

As noted earlier, there is currently a lack of empirical data on the etiology and dynamics of wifebeating. The present research had the following goals: (1) To identify factors which predispose a man to become violent towards his spouse; (2) to identify factors which precipitate the first use of violence; (3) to identify factors which facilitate or inhibit the severity, frequency, and duration of the physical abuse; (4) to collect data on the demographics, family backgrounds, personality traits, and communication patterns of violent couples; (5) to collect data on the characteristics of the violence itself (the severity, frequency, whether or not a weapon was used, etc.); (6) to identify personality types among batterers and battered women; (7) to compare battered and non-battered women on their levels of traditionalism and self-disclosure; (8) to compare violent and non-violent couples with regard to demographics, family background, man's use of alcohol, and man's arrest record; (9) to measure the battered woman's degree of satisfaction with various public and private social services.

Hypotheses

Previous research has suggested that wifebeating tends to be associated with the following factors: Violence in the man's and/or woman's family of origin; adherence to a traditional role model by the man and/or the woman; low levels of verbal communication between the man and woman; and financial problems and/or other situational stresses. Based on these findings, the following hypotheses were proposed:

Predisposing Factors

1. Men who were exposed to child abuse or wife abuse as children will be more likely to abuse their own wives than men from non-violent backgrounds.

2. Women who were exposed to child abuse or wife abuse as children will be more likely to become battered than women from non-violent homes.

3. Couples who have low verbal communication with one another will experience more violence than couples who have high verbal communication.

Factors Related to Characteristics of the Violence

1. Men who try to adhere to a rigid, traditional masculine role will be more severe and/or frequent in their violence than men who do not adhere to a rigid role model.

2. Men who try to be dominant but also display dependency on their wives will be more severe and/or frequent in their violence than men who do not exper-

ience that sort of conflict.

3. Women who adhere to a rigid, traditional feminine role model will stay in a violent situation longer than women who do not adhere to a rigid model.

4. Women with relatively low self-esteem will stay in a violent situation longer than women with relatively high self-esteem.

5. Battered women who experienced childhood violence will stay in the abusive situation longer than battered women who did not experience childhood violence.

6. Men who experience job problems and/or financial difficulties will be more severe and/or frequent in their violence than men who do not experience such problems.

7. Men who experience chronic or frequent unemployment will be more violent than men who are steadily employed.

8. The presence of domestic violence will be best predicted by a combination of the variables of exposure to childhood violence, adherence to traditional sex-role models, and degree of situational stress.

Dependent Variables

In order to fully describe the nature of the physical abuse; severity, frequency, and duration were treated as different dimensions of the violence and analyzed separately as dependent variables. A measure of the overall degree of abuse was obtained by combining the above items into an "Abuse

Score." Furthermore, it was assumed that the man would have primary control over levels of severity and frequency, while duration would be influenced more by the woman, since in the majority of cases it was she who decided when to terminate the relationship. This rationale guided the choice of factors for inclusion in the various analyses.

Method

Samples

Experimental Group (N=50). These were women with some history as victims of wifebeating. Approximately one third of the women were recruited through a local newspaper article describing this research. The remaining participants had either applied to be hot-line counselors for House of Ruth and also agreed to be in the study or were referred by friends, social service workers, or private practitioners. At the time of the interviews three of the subjects were still with their violent spouses. The others were either divorced, separated, widowed, or remarried. The women were not paid for their participation.

Comparison Group (N=50). Members of this group had non-violent marriages and were recruited from local women's organizations, church groups, and by personal referral. Each "comparison" subject was matched with an "experimental" subject on education level.

Data Collection Procedure

Interview. The investigator conducted a personal, tape recorded interview with each of the "experimental" women, except for client number 50, who was interviewed on the telephone.[22] The format of the interview was openended. Probe questions (see Appendix) were used to obtain information not spontaneously offered by the respondent. Interviews ordinarily lasted ninety minutes. Women in the Comparison Group were not interviewed.

Questionnaires. Each woman in the study answered questionnaires which were designed to: (1) Measure her relative satisfaction with various agencies (see Appendix, Questionnaire A); (2) measure her degree of traditionalism with regard to child rearing and the husband/wife relationship (see Appendix, Questionnaire B); and (3) measure the overall level of self-disclosure between the woman and her present husband or living partner (see Appendix, Questionnaire C). Women who were currently living alone did not fill out Questionnaire C (Experimental Group N=26, Control Group N=41).

Women in the Experimental Group answered the questionnaire at the end of the interview. Comparison subjects were either sent the material by mail or were questioned by telephone. Comparison women were also asked whether or not they or their husbands had been exposed to alcoholism or violence in their families of origin.

Results

Representative Case Histories

The following histories are composites of individual cases and have been included to provide a detailed, integrated description of representative couples and the progression of violence in their relationships.

1. *Janice and Donald*

Janice came from a non-violent, middle class family. Her father sold insurance, and her mother never worked outside the home. Both her parents were strict and domineering, believing that girls had to be "sheltered" from the world. Janice was, in fact, overprotected, allowed little freedom and given few responsibilities; she did not even know how to balance a checkbook when she got married. In Janice's home, it was not acceptable to show emotions. Family members were not supposed to get angry at each other. If there were a disagreement, it had to be discussed quietly, rationally, and "cooly." Janice could not remember her mother and father ever having an argument in front of her.

Although Janice said that she did not have an entirely unhappy childhood, her mother and father maintained almost total control over her until her marriage. In fact, her parents told her that she could not leave home until she *was* married, regardless of how old she was. When Janice graduated from high school, she wanted to become a social worker. Her parents wanted her to be a beautician, and informed her that if she enrolled in sociology they would not help her in any way. If she went to beauty college, however, they would pay her tuition and support her while she was in school. Although Janice was very disappointed, she felt that she had no choice but to do as her family wished.

When Janice was eighteen, and training to be a beautician, her parents would not allow her to go out on a date on the weekend unless she had "cleaned her plate" at dinner during the week. Her father also routinely opened her mail, because he believed it was his prerogative. As Janice said, "Regardless of how old I was, my parents always treated me as though I were about thirteen."When a friend introduced Janice to Donald, it was like a dream come true. Donald seemed nice, always acted like a gentleman, and seemed to provide Janice with a chance to escape from a restrictive environment.

Donald's father was a carpenter. Donald was the youngest son, and was spoiled and overprotected by his mother. Both parents gave in to Donald's temper tantrums. When Donald wanted something special, his mother would always manage to get it for him, even if the family could not really afford it. Donald's father beat his wife, and Donald remembers times when he would put a pillow over his head so that he would not hear the screaming and shouting. Donald was not abused as a child, but was never really allowed to grow up. He remained dependent upon his mother even as an adult, and frequently went to her for both financial and emotional support. His mother was not only always willing to help him, but also later blamed Janice for all of Donald's problems. Donald expressed a rather strong ambivalence toward his mother - he needed her, but also complained that she was difficult to get along with. After Donald graduated from high school he became an apprentice carpenter, following in his father's footsteps, in more ways than one.

Janice and Donald were married when they were eighteen and twenty years old, respectively. Janice loved Donald, but she married primarily to get away from home. She also felt guilty over their premarital sexual relationship. Having been raised with very strict moral standards, Janice felt she had no other choice but to marry the man she had slept with. Soon after the wedding, Janice discovered that her husband had a bad temper. When he got angry, he would throw things at her or put his fist through the wall. About five years into the marriage, Donald and Janice were sitting and having a discussion about an upcoming vacation when he suddenly lunged at her from across the room and began choking her. Janice was totally shocked by the incident, but Donald was sorry, begged forgiveness, and promised that he would never do it again. Janice wanted to believe him, so she tried to put it out of her mind. After all, it was a big responsibility for Donald to support her and their three little girls. Donald also turned out to be very jealous. He would not allow Janice to have any of her own friends, and expected her to do nothing outside of the home unless it was related to housework or the family. He also seemed to be jealous of the time she spent with the children, although he never abused them.

As time went on the beatings got worse. Janice later found out that he had been having an affair at the time the violence intensified. The battering was accompanied by verbal abuse. Donald told her she was worthless, incompetent, could not even manage a house as well as his mother, (after all, she had had five children and Janice had only three), and wondered what in the world he had done to deserve such a terrible wife. Janice's reactions to the physical and emotional abuse were twofold. First, she tended to try to deny that the violence actually happened. "I had gone right from the shelter of Mommy and Daddy to the shelter of the marriage. I lived in a dream world. I had my own idea of what Donald was like - just like my father. When he didn't live up to this image, I'd say, 'Oh well, that's not really like him, he'll come around'." Janice lived in this world for six more years, and it took its toll. Her second reaction was depression. She became like a "zombie," barely managing to do the housework and care for the children. She finally reached the point where she did not care what happened to her at all.

The violence also became more frequent. At the beginning, Donald was usually drunk when he battered her, but later he attacked her even when he was sober. During the worst period, there was an episode about once a month. Janice never knew what Donald expected to accomplish by beating her. He never told her. Janice was also unable to determine what would make him stop during a given incident. He would just suddenly stop hitting her and immediately be very sorry, almost unwilling to believe that he had caused the bruises, cuts, and other injuries. After a beating, Donald would usually want to have sexual intercourse as a way of making up. As Janice said, "If I took him into my bed, he figured he'd been forgiven, and things were all back to normal again."

After about six years of abuse, Janice decided that she would have to get out, and she went to her parents for help. Their response was that she obviously should not stay with such a man, but that she certainly could not expect to come back and live with them. She would simply have to find a job and do it on her own. At that point, Janice decided that the situation was hopeless and gave up. In fact, she later said that she might never have left if it had not been for the effect the violence was having on their children. The six-year-old withdrew and virtually stopped talking. All three had difficulty concentrating in school, and awoke often during the night, crying. For Janice the turning point came when, after a beating, she went into her children's room, and saw her nine-year-old daughter sitting in a corner, rocking and sucking her thumb.

For no other reason than to have her girls grow up normally, Janice decided that she would have to get out. When she finally told Donald about it he was distraught. He said she was a fool for breaking up their marriage, because he still loved her. He promised that he would make it up to her, and would never hit her again. When Janice refused to change her mind, Donald threatened to commit suicide, but never actually made an attempt. After the divorce, Donald went home to live with his mother, who had separated from his father two years previously. For two more years Donald wrote Janice long, pleading letters, begging her to come back. Janice still has some trouble supporting her family, but she has said that the freedom she has now is worth any amount of hard work and deprivation.

2. *Laura and David*

Laura was an only child. Her father is a professor, her mother, a secretary. Laura had a relatively happy childhood, but was never able to spend much time with her parents. Although her mother and father were loving, they were rarely involved in school activities, and Laura felt that her communication with them was not very good. Laura's home life was not at all restrictive. In fact, she was actually given a bit more responsibility than she wanted; when she was nine years old she was given a key to the house so that she could take care of herself when she came home from school. Although her mother tended to have a bad temper, there was no violence or verbal abuse. Laura described herself as an independent person and somewhat of a rebel. "I'm a fighter, not a quitter." Laura met David when she was a freshman in college. He was working in the cafeteria. Both of their families thought they were too young to get married. Laura's parents did not feel that David's background was comparable to hers, and did not attend the wedding.

Although there had been no violence in David's family, his father was a successful contractor, who always criticized David and "put him down." David constantly competed with his father, and felt that he could never satisfy parental expectations. When David was a sophomore in high school, he was beaten up by some other boys, and felt totally humiliated by the experience. During the next two years he took weight lifting and body building to increase his strength. He then sought out the same boys and took revenge. Laura felt that David had always been insecure about his own masculinity. David said that he liked to pick fights because he knew he would usually win. David would also frequently lie about past exploits, exaggerating his strength and belligerence. Once he even bought himself a karate outfit, "practiced" in the backyard, boasting to others that he was a blackbelt. David never had a karate lesson in his life.

Laura got her first beating about one year after the wedding, when David, who worked as a sales clerk, lost his job. The violence between Laura and David was almost invariably preceded by an argument of some sort. Laura was articulate, and more intelligent than her spouse. Although David sometimes abused Laura verbally, she never really believed him. She knew that she was not only an adequate wife and mother, but also a good provider, since she was the one who worked steadily. Laura also handled all the money because David was not responsible enough to do it.

At the beginning, beatings would occur about once every six weeks, and were never very severe. David would sometimes throw her up against a wall and Laura usually got a few bruises. David always seemed to use violence for a specific reason, such as to win an argument. After he felt he had asserted himself properly, he would stop. Laura was convinced that beatings were directly related to his desire to be the "dominant male," since the abuse increased in frequency when her husband was unemployed. It was not uncommon for their friends to witness the violence. However, they generally sided with David, saying that Laura should be a more traditional, submissive wife, regardless of who was earning the money. David also maintained that the battering was Laura's fault - he only became violent because she had done something wrong, had not obeyed him, or was not a good enough wife.

Laura said that once the abuse began, their relationship deteriorated quite quickly. Communication nearly ceased entirely, and her sexual desire greatly diminished. After a violent incident David would want to have sexual relations, and Laura felt that he used intercourse as another means of dominating her and asserting himself. Laura reported that she felt she had been raped several times during the marriage.

They had one little boy, whom David generally ignored and neglected. Laura also called the police several times, and they could usually calm him down. After about three years of marriage, Laura felt that things would never get better. The violence was starting to occur about every two or three weeks, and David seemed more and more compulsive about being dominant and getting his way. Laura filed for divorce and moved out. However, David even harassed her during the separation. In fact, he gave her the most severe beating after the divorce was final. David hit her in the face and split her lip seriously enough to require stitches. At this point, Laura decided to file charges. She called the police, made a statement, and went to the district attorney. However, the D.A. refused to do anything about it. Laura reported feeling more anger and bitterness about the lack of police and legal response than she did about David's violence. She is currently living with a man, but is still quite wary about getting remarried.

3. *Marcia and Peter*

Marcia had a tragic childhood. Her father, whom she adored, died when she was eight. Her mother subsequently remarried a violent alcoholic, who battered both his wife and his own children. Marcia lived in such fear for her mother, that she would even hide the knives from her stepfather when he came home drunk. Although Marcia herself was never beaten, she was sexually abused by her stepfather. When she was about fifteen, Marcia finally had the courage to tell a school counselor what had been happening at home. Her mother and stepfather denied everything and punished Marcia severely. The authorities never took any further action. Marcia desperately wanted to get away from home, and when she met Peter, she saw her chance. Unfortunately, it didn't work out quite as she had anticipated.

Peter, too, had had a difficult childhood. His father was an alcoholic, and Peter was sometimes sent into bars to look for his father and plead with him to come home. When Peter was nine years old, his father deserted the family. His mother remarried a year later and put Peter in military school. However, she let his two younger sisters stay with her and her new husband. Peter never forgave his mother for sending him away.

The violence erupted about two years into the marriage. Peter had been working in the yard and asked Marcia to fix lunch for him. When she said that she would do it in a few minutes, he picked up one of the tools he was working with, threw it at her, and hit her in the back. After that first incident, Peter never used a weapon again, but the violence did become quite severe. During one episode he tore the phone off the wall, and completely ripped off a sliding screen door. Marcia also suffered a broken jaw when he threw her to the ground one time during an argument.

As time went on, the assaults became more severe, more frequent, and more random. Toward the end of their relationship, the episodes were totally unpredictable. When Peter came home from work Marcia never knew whether he would be in a good mood or whether he would hit her.

Peter had a "responsible position" in the community and was therefore very "image conscious." He was careful never to hit Marcia, or even argue with her in public. In fact, Peter usually attempted to deny his own violence. During one beating, he gave Marcia a black eye and severely bruised one side of her face. However, when she confronted him the next day he insisted that, "You ran into my fist, I didn't hit you."

At one point Marcia did go to her minister - he gave her a Bible, and told her that as a Christian she should forgive her husband. Although Marcia never really could forgive Peter, she rarely expressed her anger outwardly. As a result, she developed an ulcer and became dependent on tranquilizers.

Peter never apologized for his violence, and expected everything to be back to normal the next day. If the children had seen it happen, Marcia always "covered up" for him saying, "Well, Daddy was mad." If the children had not directly witnessed it, she would tell them that she fell down or had hurt herself in some other way. Marcia said one of the reasons that she stayed was that she was "Florence Nightingale from the word go." Although Peter himself never admitted that he had a problem, it was clear to her that he needed her help. She was convinced that her love would transform him into a non-violent loving person.

Marcia worked as a secretary during most of the marriage, but Peter handled the money and she had to turn her paycheck over to him. Although at the time she felt that she probably could have made it on her own, she did not want a divorce because it would have meant that she was a failure as a person and that no one would ever love her. As time went on, Marcia became desperate. One day, Peter was working on the car, lying down in front of the wheels. Marcia was in the car, and thought to herself how easy it would be to simply take the brake off, run over him, and claim it was an accident. These feelings were so strong that it frightened her, and she felt that if she didn't leave then, she might really end up killing him. Peter begged her to stay, but did not bother her during the separation or contest the divorce. Their marriage had lasted thirteen years. Peter has subsequently remarried twice, and Marcia knows for certain that there was violence in his second marriage. Marcia has been very happily remarried for four years.

4. *Ruth and Joe*

Ruth was one of ten children in a poor family. Her father was an unskilled laborer who did odd jobs, and the family barely survived economically. Ruth was raised very strictly, and remembers feeling some anger and hostility toward her mother. Children in the family were never allowed to talk back to parents or even to disagree with them. There was no violence in her background, but Ruth recalls her childhood was not particularly happy. She met Joe in high school, and at the beginning, he was very nice to her. However, he was also very jealous and possessive; she was *his* girl and nobody was allowed to touch her. Ruth had never been very popular with boys, so she was very flattered by this attention. After they had been dating for about six months, Ruth discovered that she was pregnant. When she told Joe, he was happy, and seemed to want both the child and the marriage. Ruth, too, was satisfied with the arrangement at first. However, about a month before the wedding the two were having an argument and Joe hit her across the face. Although his violence frightened Ruth, she felt she had no choice but to marry. Since she was Catholic, she could not get an abortion, and she knew that her family could never take care of her and her child. Ruth was sixteen when she and Joe were married.

Joc's father was a construction worker who drank heavily, but was not violent to his wife. The oldest of six children, Joe was always held responsible for his brothers and sisters, and was beaten with a belt if younger ones did not behave properly. Joe always resented this, and felt that he had been treated unfairly. When Joe graduated from high school he became a truck driver.

After the wedding, Ruth discovered that her fears had been well founded. Joe began to drink heavily, and when he was drunk he became violent. In the past few years Joe's alcohol use has increased and his behavior has become more irrational and erratic. If Joe goes out drinking and Ruth keeps his dinner warm for him, he accuses her of having fixed it for her lover, and he beats her. If she does not keep his dinner warm, he calls her a lazy, good-for-nothing bitch who does not take care of her husband, and beats her. Afterwards he is somewhat apologetic, but he always adds, "Why did you make me do it? If only you wouldn't act that way, I wouldn't get so angry. You are the only person in the world who could make me do this."

Ruth has left Joe several times, but she always comes back. She has told several people about the violence and they all suggest that she get a divorce. However, she has never worked, has no job skills, and would not be able to support herself and her five children. Ruth applied for welfare once, but found the forms and requirements confusing, and the delays, frustrating. Ruth also said that it would hurt her pride to be on welfare. She simply could not bear the shame of taking a "handout."

When Joe is not drinking, he is generally very nice to his family. Ruth has also found that she can sometimes avert an attack if she is submissive and acquiescent. Although Joe never wants to have sexual intercourse after a beating, if at other times Ruth is not interested, he insists, even using force to get her to comply with his wishes. The violence in this relationship has been rather severe; Ruth has had her arm and two ribs broken, but has never been hospitalized. Joe has never thrown things or destroyed inanimate objects. As Ruth said, "Joe much prefers to beat upon on me instead of something as dull as a chair or a table."

Ruth and Joe have been married for twenty years, and all of their children have emotional problems. Their oldest boy is hostile and aggressive and has already been arrested for petty theft. Their fifteen-year-old daughter is pregnant, unmarried, and living at home. Although Ruth has not been beaten in the last eight months, she is afraid that the only reason he has not attacked her is because he is currently on parole for drunken driving. Joe is well aware that if he hits her she will call the police and he would go to jail. Both Ruth and I were worried about what would happen in two months when Joe's parole ended.

Quantitative Analyses

Demographics

Race. In the Experimental Group, 48 of the women were White, one was Black, and one was Mexican-American. Forty-five of the men were White, two were Black, two were Mexican-American, and one was Mexican-American Indian. All men and women in the Control Group were White.

Religion. In the Experimental Group the most represented religion was Catholicism (22% of both men and women), but no religion predominated. However, there was a positive correlation between a woman's being a Catholic or Mormon and staying a relatively long time in the marriage ($r = +.37$, p less than .02). In addition, men who were either Catholic or Mormon were more frequent in their violence than men who had other religious affiliations or "no preference" in their beliefs ($r = +.35$, p less than .01). Men were twice as likely as women to have had no preference in religious affiliation.

A similar distribution of religious affiliation was found in the Control Group, with 24% (men and women combined) listing Catholicism as their religion (See Table 1).

Prior Marriages. In both the Experimental and Control Groups, the majority of both men and women had not been married prior to the relationship under study. Among violent couples where there had been prior marriages, 3 of 9 women had experienced violence in the first marriage. By comparison, there were 14 men who had been married before, and there was no known violence in nine of these cases. In the other five cases the women did not know whether or not there had been violence (See Table 2).

Number of Children. Seventy-four percent of the families had two or less children. In 6% of the cases the couple had six or more children. The average number of children was three. There was no significant difference between the Experimental and Control Groups with regard to family size.

Characteristics of the Violence

Frequency. Eight percent of the women left their husbands after the first beating, and the violence remained at the same level throughout the relationship in 12% of the cases (see Table 3). In all other instances the frequency increased over time. The modal frequency during the least violent period was once a month, and during the most violent period, once a week (see Table 3). There was a wide range in the degree of increase in frequency. In the least case, the violence became 1-1/3 times more frequent during the relationship. The greatest increase reported was one case in which the violence had become sixty times more frequent (see Table 4). There was no significant relationship between frequency and severity or between frequency and the number of years a

Table 1

Religious Affiliation Among Men and Women in Experimental and Control Groups

	Percent of Cases			
	Experimental Group		Control Group	
	Women	Men	Women	Men
Catholic	11	22	26	20
Protestant	18	22	22	24
Baptist	14	6	4	2
Methodist	8	4	10	10
Lutheran	4	2	4	2
Presbyterian	4	0	4	6
Episcopalian	4	0	2	2
Church of Christ	2	2	0	2
Religious Science	2	0	2	0
Mormon	2	0	0	6
Quaker	0	2	0	0
Pentecostal	0	0	0	2
Jewish	4	2	4	4
Christian Science	0	0	2	0
Atheist	2	8	0	0
No preference	14	30	20	20

Table 2

Prior Marriages Among Men and Women

In Experimental and Control Groups

	Percent of Cases Number of Prior Marriages			
Experimental Group	None	1	2	3
Men	70	24	4	2
Women	84	16	0	0
Control Group				
Men	86	10	4	0
Women	78	22	0	0

Table 3

Frequency of Violence

	Percent of Cases		
	Cases in Which Frequency Increased[a]		
	Least Violent Period	Most Violent Period	Cases in Which Frequency Did Not Increase[b]
Once a year	2	0	0
Every six months	12	2	0
Every three months	12	2	50
Every two months	6	4	0
Every six weeks	4	0	17
Once a month	22	12	17
Every three weeks	0	6	17
Every two weeks	0	8	0
Once a week	8	16	0
Daily	0	12	0
Unpredictable	12	16	0
Only one incident	8	8	0

a. N = 44

b. N = 6

Table 4

Degree of Increase in Frequency

Degree	Percent of Cases
1-1/3 times as frequent	2
2 times as frequent	12
3 times as frequent	12
4 times as frequent	12
4-1/3 times as frequent	2
6 times as frequent	4
7 times as frequent	6
8 times as frequent	2
12 times as frequent	2
30 times as frequent	2
60 times as frequent	2
Only one incident	8
No increase in frequency	12
Always unpredictable	12
Unpredictable to every three weeks	2
Unpredictable to weekly	2
Unpredictable to daily	2
Every three months to unpredictable	2
Every six weeks to unpredictable	2

woman experienced violence.

A more precise measure of the degree of increase in frequency was obtained by assigning each case a score based on the average number of violent incidents a year. The score for the least frequent period was then subtracted from the score of the most frequent period. There was a negative correlation between the degree of increase and the man's experiencing job problems ($r = -.36$, p less than .02).

Severity. A scale from one to seven was developed to measure the severity of the physical abuse at its highest intensity. The degree of severity was determined by two factors: (1) The extent of the injuries suffered by the woman, and (2) whether or not the man ever used a weapon against his wife. For example, a score of three indicates that the man used his fists to cause bruises - but no broken bones - and either choked the woman or used a weapon at some time. In only two cases was the violence scored as one (not severe). The Average score was three (see Table 5). In 78% of the cases women indicated that the severity of the violence increased over time. Furthermore, there was a positive correlation between severity and the number of years women experienced abuse ($r = +.25$, p less than .03).

Increases in Levels of Violence. In the majority of cases both frequency (88%) and severity (88%) increased over time. The violence did not increase in either frequency or severity in only 6% of the cases. Frequency alone remained at the same level in 6% of the cases, and severity alone did not increase in another 6% of the cases.

Abuse Score. In order to obtain an overall measure of abuse, cases were assigned a score of one for "high" and a zero for "low" on each of the dimensions of severity, frequency, and duration. These scores were then summed. The

Table 5

Severity of Violence

Degree	Description	% of Cases
	1. Slaps with open hand	4
Moderately	2. Uses fists, causes bruises	26
Severe	3. Uses fists, causes bruises, and chokes woman or uses a weapon	22
	4. Causes broken bones, concussion, or injuries requiring stitches	30
Severe	5. Causes broken bones, concussion, or injuries requiring stitches and uses weapon	6
Very	6. Woman hospitalized	10
Severe	7. Woman hospitalized and weapon used	2

resulting abuse scores were normally distributed, and there was a positive correlation between the degree of increase and overall abuse ($r = +.41$, p less than .01) (see Table 6).

Generality of the Violence. Fifty-two percent of the men were violent toward inanimate objects either between beatings or during an incident. In 36% of the cases the man's violence extended to individuals outside the immediate family, and in 18% of the cases men abused one or more of their children at least once. Sixteen percent of the men were chronic child abusers (see Table 7). Furthermore, not a single woman had attempted to stop her husband's chronic mistreatment of their children. Only two women ever brought charges against their spouses for child abuse.

Drunkenness. Twenty percent of the women reported that their husbands were always drunk when violence occurred, while 16% of the men were never drunk when the beatings occurred. Only two women said that they themselves had usually been drinking at the time of an incident (see Table 8).

Weapons. Fourteen percent of the women reported that their husbands had threatened them with a gun. In 8% of those cases the man did actually shoot his wife.

"Blind Rage". Thirty-four percent of the women said that their husbands would always go into a "blind rage" during a beating. Another 32% would go into a "blind rage" only on some occasions. Furthermore, there was a positive correlation between going into a "blind rage" and the severity of the violence ($r = +52$, p less than .001), and with the overall level of abuse ($r = +32$, p less than .03).

Pattern. Forty-two percent of the women said that they had been unable to discern any particular pattern to the

Table 6

Overall Abuse[a] Scores[b]

	Percent of Cases
Low on all dimensions	12
Low on two dimensions, high on one	38
Low on one dimension, high on two	36
High on all dimensions	14

a. Based on dimensions of severity, frequency, and duration.
b. Cases in which one element was "unpredictable" were assigned the average score.

Table 7

Incidence of Child Abuse Among Violent Couples

	Percent of Cases
Never	56
One Incident by man	12
Chronic abuse by man	16
Chronic abuse by both man and woman	2
One incident by man; chronic abuse by woman	2
Couple had no children during period of violence	12

Table 8

Incidence of Man's Drunkenness When Violent

Frequency	Percent of Cases
Never	16
Rarely	12
Sometimes	24
Usually	26
Always	20
Couldn't tell	2

violence. In 18% of the cases the beatings were always related to the same specific reason such as the woman's "flirting." Twenty-two percent of the beatings occurred on a time cycle, with incidents coming once every three weeks, for example. There was but one incident of violence in 8% of the cases, and 4% of the women reported that they were beaten anytime they said "no" to their husbands' demands.

Reason for the Violence. Twenty-six percent of the women indicated that they never really knew what their husbands expected to accomplish by being violent. In 12% of the cases, women reported the beatings were always associated with the same specific problem such as their "flirting" or being a bad housekeeper, while another 8% said their husbands employed physical force as a means of winning arguments. Thirty-two percent of the women felt that men used the abuse in order to achieve total domination and control over them. Furthermore, there was a positive correlation between using violence to achieve control and the severity of the abuse ($r = +38$, p less than .02), the man's level of expressed hostility ($r = +48$, p less than .01), and with his overall level of alcohol consumption ($r = +38$, p less than .02). There was a negative correlation between a man's using violence for domination and his having job problems ($r = -.32$, p less than .05).

Reactions to the Violence

Remorse. Only 22% of the men ordinarily expressed extreme remorse after a beating. Forty percent of the husbands expressed only mild remorse, and even then did not consistently apologize. Thirty-eight percent never expressed any remorse whatsoever. Fifty-six percent of the women reported that their husbands seemed to have made a special effort to be nice to them for a period immediately following a beating.

Post-Violent Sex. Forty-six percent of the women reported that their husbands never wanted to have sexual intercourse immediately after a beating. Eight percent wanted sex on a few occasions, and 40% of the men usually wanted sexual relations afterward. In the remaining 14% of the cases, beatings were always directly related to the man's desire for sexual intercourse or for a specific sex act. Half of the women felt that their husbands' interest in sex represented a genuine desire to "make up," and half felt that the men used intercourse as another means of achieving domination.

Medical Attention. Sixty-eight percent of the women either consulted a private physician or went to the hospital for treatment of injuries.

Discussion of Violence. Twenty-eight percent of the women never discussed the violence with their husbands, and 54% of the women never told anyone about the violence during the time the abuse was taking place. Women who did talk about the problem were more likely to have confided in a friend than a family member.

Psychological Effects. Seventy-six percent of the women reported that they felt embarrassed because they were beaten. Sixty-six percent said that they felt ashamed about the violence. Thirty-two percent of the women suffered from psychosomatic illnesses during the marriage or relationship. Seventy-eight percent reported that they had become severely depressed at some time. Eighteen percent of the women had attempted suicide at least once.

Reaction to Woman's Leaving. When it became clear that their wives were really going to leave, five men threatened to commit suicide, three other men attempted suicide but did not succeed, and two men killed themselves. Although 26% of the men begged their wives to stay, 32% made no effort to keep their wives from leaving. Twenty percent of the men either "hassled" or beat their wives after the divorce. Men who made an effort to stop their wives from leaving were also likely to have been drunk when violent ($r = +.45$, p less than .001). There was a negative correlation between trying to convince the wife to stay and the previous severity of the violence ($r = -.37$, p less than .004), and the overall abuse ($r = -.34$, p less than .001).

Possible Predisposing Factors

Status Inequality. In the Experimental Group, the socio-economic level for women tended to be higher than that for men. Forty-six percent of the women came from families where the father was either a professional or held a managerial position. Twenty-two percent were craftsmen, and 12% were unskilled. By contrast, only 24% of the men came from professional or managerial families. In addition, 22% of these fathers were unskilled laborers, and 22% were craftsmen. Women also tended to experience downward mobility with marriage; only 32% of the husbands were professionals or managers. Although more Experimental Group women were currently employed than Control Group women (Chi Square = 20.6, df = 4, p less than .001), there was no significant difference between violent and non-violent men with regard to occupation level (see Table 9).

In the Experimental Group, 54% of the women had had a higher education level than their husbands. Twenty-two percent of the couples had completed an equal number of years of education, and 24% of the wives had less education than their husbands. By contrast, fewer women in the Control Group than in the Experimental Group had achieved a

Table 9
Current Occupations Among Men and Woman
In Experimental and Control Groups, and Occupations of the
Fathers and Fathers-in-Law Among Experimental Group Women

	Percent of Cases					
	Experimental Group				Control Group	
	Woman's Current Occupation	Woman's Father's Occupation	Man's Father's Occupation	Man's Current Occupation	Man's Current Occupation	Woman's Current Occupation
Professional	24	16	10	4	14	2
Managerial	12	30	14	24	24	4
Clerical	36	6	2	2	2	18
Military or Police	0	6	2	2	0	0
Sales	2	4	4	12	20	20
Craft	8	24	22	26	16	2
Unskilled	0	12	24	22	8	10
Rarely Employed	0	2	8	6	0	0
Unemployed	18	0	2	2	4	44
Missing Data	0	0	12	0	12	0

higher education level than their husbands (Chi Square = 20.19, df = 2, p less than .0001) (See Table 10).

Education Level. In the Experimental Group, 24% of the women and 28% of the men had achieved only high school diplomas. Eighteen percent of the women and 16% of the men had college degrees or post graduate degrees. By contrast, 22% of the men in the Control Group had high school diplomas and 42% had college or post graduate degrees. There was a significant difference between the education levels of the violent and non-violent men (Chi Square = 10.72, df = 1, p less than .01).

Age Married. In the Experimental Group, 72% of the women were married or entered into a relationship with a man at 21 years old or younger. By contrast, only 14% of the men were 21 years old or younger at the time of the marriage. There was no statistically significant difference between battered and non-battered women with regard to age when married (See Table 11).

Alcohol Consumption. Thirty-eight percent of the battered women rated their husbands as alcoholics, while 22% of the men were described as "heavy drinkers." Not surprisingly, there was a positive correlation between heavy alcohol use and being drunk when violent (r = +.34, p less than .007).

The non-violent men had a lower level of alcohol consumption than the violent men (Chi Square = 7.84, df = 2, p less than .05). When women in the Experimental Group were asked about their own present level of alcohol use, one reported that she was an alcoholic, and one that she was a "heavy drinker." There were no significant differences between battered and non-battered women with regard to their use of liquor (See Table 12).

Table 10

Education Level and Status Inequality
In Experimental and Control Groups

Level Completed	Experimental Group Women	Experimental Group Men	Control[a] Group Men
Did not complete high school	6	28	6
High school graduate	24	28	22
1 to 3 years college	52	28	30
BA degree	14	12	30
Post Graduate degree	4	4	12

Education Level	Percent of Cases Experimental Group	Percent of Cases Control Group
Woman less educated than man	24	40
Woman and man equally educated	22	48
Woman more educated than man	54	12

a. Battered and non-battered women were matched on education level.

Table 11

Age Married - Experimental and Control Groups

	Percent of Cases			
	Experimental Group		Control Group	
Age	Women	Men	Women	Men
12 - 16	8	0	4	0
17 - 21	64	46	74	48
22 - 25	18	26	16	40
26 - 30	8	16	6	4
31 - 35	2	8	0	6
36 - 40	0	2	0	2
41 - 50	0	2	0	0

Table 12

Alcohol Use Among Men and Women
In Experimental and Control Groups

	Percent of Use			
Level	Experimental Group		Control Group	
of Use	Women	Men	Women	Men
None	20	4	16	20
Social	62	20	68	58
Moderate	14	16	16	18
Heavy	2	22	0	0
Alcoholic	2	38	0	4

Drug Use. Twenty-four percent of the Experimental Group women said that their husbands used marijuana socially. Another 26% of the men used pills regularly. None of the men appeared to have been addicted to "hard drugs." Twenty percent of the women reported ever using marijuana, 4%, pills. One woman had been addicted to heroin for a period during the marriage. By contrast, only 8% of the women in the Control Group reported they had ever used marijuana, and 10% reported that their husbands had ever used marijuana. None of the respondents in the Control Group had ever been dependent on pills.

Man's Arrest Record. Sixty-six percent of the violent men had been arrested at least once during the marriage or within one year of the separation. The most common reason for arrest was drunken driving. Only two men were ever charged with wifebeating. Fewer men in the Control Group were ever arrested than men in the Experimental Group (Chi Square = 35.7, df = 1, p less than .0001) (see Table 13).

Family Background. The majority of both men (56%) and women (66%) in the Experimental Group had not been exposed to violence in their families or origin (see Table 14). However, men who had experienced childhood violence were later more severe in their wife abuse than men from non-violent backgrounds (r = +.25, p less than .04), and also tended to be violent to individuals outside the immediate family (r = +.26, p less than .04). Finally, with regard to childhood violence in the Control Group, fewer men (Chi Square = 19.79, df = 1, p less than .0001) and fewer women (Chi Square = 10.56, df = 1, p less than .001) had been exposed to violence than in the Experimental Group.

The majority of men (76%) and women (80%) in the Experimental Group had not been exposed to alcoholism in their families of origin (see Table 14). In the control Group,

Table 13

Arrest Record for Experimental Group Men[a]

Charges	Percent of Cases
Drunk driving	20
Drunk and disorderly	6
Drunk driving and theft	2
Drunk driving and wifebeating (wife pressed)	2
Assault and battery (not pressed by wife)	10
Kidnapping (wife pressed)	2
Assault and kidnapping (wife pressed)	2
Child stealing and molesting (wife pressed)	2
Child abuse and battery (wife pressed)	2
Auto theft	2
Receiving stolen goods	2
Possession of drugs	4
Homicide (not pressed by wife)	2
Breaking and entering	2
Juvenile arrests	2
Non-payment of traffic tickets	4
Never arrested	34

a. No men in the Control Group were ever arrested.

Table 14

Violence and Alcoholism in Family of Origin

Among Men and Women in Experimental

and Control Group

	Percent of Cases			
	Experimental Group		Control Group	
Violence	Women	Men	Women	Men
None	66	56	94	96
Wife abuse	10	28	2	4
Child abuse	14	4	2	0
Wife and child abuse	10	12	2	0
Alcoholism				
None	80	76	88	90
Father	14	20	8	6
Mother	4	2	0	2
Both	2	2	4	2

92% of the men and 90% of the women came from homes where there was no alcoholism.

With regard to general characteristics of the family background, 82% of the "experimental" women said that they had been raised strictly. Furthermore, there was a positive correlation between having had a strict upbringing and remaining for a relatively long period in the violent marriage ($r = +.26$, p less than .04). In addition, women who reported having felt unloved as children were more likely to believe their husband's verbal abuse than women who did not feel unloved as children ($r = +.28$, p less than .02).

It would also appear that the majority of batterers and their wives had not enjoyed a particularly good relationship with their parents; seventy-two percent of the women indicated that they had had poor or low communication with parents, and 62% of the women described their relationships with their mothers as having been either "not good," or "very bad." Finally, 60% of the respondents reported that their husbands had at some time expressed dislike or hatred for their own mothers.

There was a negative correlation between a woman's reporting that her husband's mother had overprotected him as a child and (1) his later use of violence to achieve total domination ($r = -.33$, p less than .04), (2) the severity of his violence ($r = -.27$, p less than .03), (3) the overall abuse ($r = -.35$, p less than .01), and (4) his level of dominance ($r = -.24$, p less than .05).

Reason for Marrying. Forty percent of the women reported that they had married for love; the men had been kind and non-violent during the courtship. Furthermore, there was a positive correlation between having married for love, and the length of the relationship ($r = +.36$, p less than .03).

However, 18% of the respondents said pregnancy was the most important motivating factor, and 12% said that they married primarily in order to get away from home (See Table 15).

Personality Factors - Experimental and Control Groups

Traditionalism. Items one through four on the Attitude Questionnaire (Questionnaire B, see Appendix) were used to obtain a measure of traditionalism in childrearing attitudes. Scores were assigned as follows: Strongly Agree = 1; Agree = 2; Undecided = 3; Disagree = 4; Strongly Disagree = 5. Scores between four and twelve were rated as "high" in traditionalism, scores between thirteen and twenty, "low." Sixteen percent of the women in the Experimental Group were rated "high," and 26% of the women in the Control Group were rated "high" in their traditionalism in child-rearing practices. The difference was not statistically significant.

Items five through nine of the Attitude Questionnaire were scored as described above, and used to reflect the level of traditionalism with regard to the marital relationship. Scores between five and fifteen were rated "high," scores between sixteen and twenty-five, rated as "low" in traditionalism. Sixty-six percent of the battered women and 78% of the non-battered women were rated "high" on traditionalism in their attitudes toward the marital relationship. The difference between groups was statistically significant ($t = 2.46$, $df = 16$, p less than .02).

Self-Disclosure. A measure of the amount of self-disclosure for both men and women in both groups was obtained by scoring and summing the responses on Questionnaire C (see Appendix) as follows: "I have lied or misrepresented myself" = -1; "I have told nothing" = 0; "I have talked

Table 15

Woman's Primary Reason for Marrying

Experimental Group

	Percent of Cases
Never married	4
Love - Man was nice to her before marriage	40
Pregnancy	18
Pressure from man to get married	6
Guilt over pre-marital sex	8
Desire to leave home	12
Couldn't give a reason	4
Convenience	8

in general terms" = 1; and "I have talked in full and complete detail" = 2. The scores ranged from zero to twenty, with scores of zero to ten rated "low" in self-disclosure, eleven to twenty as "high." Twenty-seven percent of the battered women and 25% of the non-battered women were rated "low" in self-disclosure. In the Experimental Group 23% of the women judged their current husbands to be "low" in self-disclosure, while 30% of the Control Group women perceived their husbands to be "low" in self-disclosure. When scores on self-disclosure levels for both groups were combined, there was a positive correlation between the woman's level of self-disclosure and her husband's reported level of self-disclosure (r = +.85, p less than .001).

Personality Factors - Experimental Group. Each woman in the Experimental Group was asked to describe her husband's personality. The adjectives reported were those used spontaneously by the women. Of all the adjectives mentioned, "jealous," "dominating," "insecure," and "macho" were chosen by the majority of women (see Table 16). Furthermore, men who were described as "dominating" were more severe in their violence than men not so described (Chi Square = 6.20, df = 1, p less than .01), while men who were "sweet" tended to be less severe than men who were not "sweet" (Chi Square = 4.23, df = 1, p less than .04). Finally, women who were married to men who were "cold," (Chi Square = 5.89, df = 2, p less than .04), while women whose husbands could be charming to other people stayed longer than women whose husbands were not so described (Chi Square = 6.69, df = 2, p less than .02).

Personality Scales

Man's Hostitlity. A measure of the man's hostility toward his wife was obtained by assigning a score of one for

Table 16

Woman's Description of Man's Personality

Experimental Group

	Percent of Cases
Jealous	72
Dominating	60
Insecure	54
Macho	52
Charming & friendly with others	48
Sick, disturbed, crazy	42
Selfish and demanding	42
Moody	38
Cold	34
Dr. Jekyl and Mr. Hyde	28
Tender	28
Withdrawn and aloof	26
Intelligent	24
Sadistic	22
Sweet	20
Wild	18
A ladies' man	18
Depressive	16
A woman hater	16
Manic-depressive	12
Quiet	12
Compulsive	10
Behavior change due to drugs	8

"no" and two for "yes" on the following items: (1) verbal abuse occurs during beatings and at other times as well, (2) man does other things designed to "get at" his wife, and (3) man humiliates or purposely embarrasses his wife in public. Scores were then summed, with scores of three and four being "low," five and six, "high." Fifty percent of the men were rated "high" in hostility. In addition, there was a positive correlation between the man's hostility level and the severity of his violence (r = +.42, p less than .001), the overall level of abuse (r = +36, p less than .01), and the woman's perception that violence was used to achieve total domination rather than for a specific reason such as to win an argument (r = +.48, p less than .01).

Man's Dominance. A measure of the man's dominance was obtained by assigning the number one for "no" and two for "yes" on these items: (1) man described as "dominating," (2) woman must ask husband for every penny she spends, (3) woman perceives her husband as using violence to achieve total dominance over her, (4) woman has no "say" in major decision making, and (5) man handles all the money. These scores were then summed. A score of five through seven was rated as "low," eight through ten, "high." Fifty-eight percent of the men were rated as being "low" in dominance.

There was a positive correlation between dominance and the severity of the violence (r = +.50, p less than .001), the degree of his overall physical abuse (r = +.26, p less than .03), hostility level (r = +.28, p less than .02), and being violent to individuals outside the immediate family (r = +.24, p less than .04). There was a negative correlation between a man's level of dominance and his attempting to convince his wife not to leave (r = -.39, p less than .003).

"Coldness" Scale. There was a positive correlation between being described as "cold" and also being described as

"withdrawn," "sadistic," and "selfish." A score of one was assigned for "no," and two for "yes" on each of the items including "cold," and all four items were then summed. Scores of four and five were rated "low," and six to eight, "high." Seventy-four percent of the men were "low," 26% "high." There was a positive correlation between a man's "coldness" and the frequency of his violence ($r = +.36$, p less than .01).

Precipitating Factors - The First Incident

The first violent incident occurred before the marriage in 24% of the cases. The violence began within the first year of marriage in 46% of the cases. However, one woman reported that the first abuse occurred eleven years into the marriage, and another, fifteen years. Some type of stress (e.g. job loss) was present in 80% of the cases, and 56% of the women said that a verbal argument had preceded the first violent episode (see Table 17).

Possible Facilitating Factors

Financial Problems. Fifty-four percent of the couples had faced financial difficulties at some time during the marriage, and there was a negative correlation between the presence of financial problems and the length of the marriage ($r = -.27$, p less than .03).

Job Problems. In 52% of the cases the man had had problems with his job at some time during the marriage.

Employment. Sixty-eight percent of the women were employed for some period during the marriage. Eighty-two percent of the men were "generally employed."

Table 17

Characteristics of the First Violent Incident

When did first incident occur?	Percent of Cases
Before marriage	24
1-4 weeks into marriage or relationship	8
1-5 months into marriage or relationship	8
6 months into marriage or relationship	16
1 year into marriage or relationship	16
2 years into marriage or relationship	8
3 years into marriage or relationship	8
4 years into marriage or relationship	2
5-9 years into marriage or relationship	6
10-15 years into marriage or relationship	4
Preceded by verbal argument?	
No	42
Yes	56
Couldn't remember	2
Situational stresses present?	
Job loss	34
Financial difficulties	6
Pregnancy	16
Birth of child	12
Other	12

Verbal Argument. A verbal argument always preceded the violence in 34% of the cases, and sometimes preceded the beatings in 28% of the cases. A verbal argument was more likely to precede violence in couples where the wife had achieved a higher education level than her husband (r = +.32, p less than .01).

Reasons for Staying. The most frequent reason given by women for remaining in a violent situation was that they felt sorry for their husbands. Furthermore, there was a positive correlation between women who indicated one of the reasons for staying was that they still loved their husbands, and remaining longer in the relationship (r = +.29, p less than .03). There was also a positive correlation between giving economic reasons (e.g. not being able to support herself) for staying with a husband, and remaining longer in the relationship (r = +.46, p less than .01) (see Tables 18 and 19).

Possible Inhibiting Factors

Witnesses. The violent episodes were witnessed at least once in 68% of the cases. Although the most likely witness(es) were the couple's children, friends and neighbors were also sometimes present (see Table 20). However, only four women reported that witnesses ever tried to intervene on their behalf.

Police Involvement. In 68% of the cases police had been summoned at least once. Ordinarily, it was the woman herself who made the call (see Table 21).

Why Beating Stopped. Fifty-two percent of the women said that they never knew exactly what made their husbands stop beating them during a given episode. However, 16% of the women had always been able to end a beating by giving a

Table 18

Woman's Reasons for Staying with Her Husband

Experimental Group

		Percent of Cases[a]
Economic	No way to support herself	32
	Has job, but salary too low	26
Fear	Believes he could find her anywhere	18
	Man made threats to harm her if she left	18
Social	Stigma of divorce	30
	Wants to avoid parental reaction of "I told you so"	32
Personal	Feels incapable of surviving on her own	30
	Feels sorry for man	46
	Believes man will reform	38
	Believes violence is primarily her fault	28
	Still loves the man	20

a. Women usually gave more than one reason for staying.

Table 19

Combination of Reasons for Staying

	Percent of Cases
Personal only	16
Social only	8
Economic only	4
Economic and Personal	12
Fear and Personal	4
Fear and Economic	2
Economic and Social	6
Social and Personal	10
Social, Economic, and Personal	22
Social, Economic, Personal, and Fear	4
Economic, Personal, and Fear	10

Table 20

Cases In Which At Least One Incident Of Violence Was Witnessed

Witnesses	Percent of Cases
None	32
Children	22
Other family member	6
Neighbor or friend	6
More than one witness[a]	34

a. Combination of two or more of the above categories.

Table 21

Cases In Which Police Were Called

	Percent of Cases
None	36
Other family member called once	4
Neighbor called once	8
Woman called once	22
Woman called two or more times	30

"cue" such as crying or pretending to faint (see Table 22). It is also interesting to note that none of the women who could reliably stop a beating reported that their husbands used violence as a means of achieving total domination.

Pregnancy. Of the 38 women who had had pregnancies during the period of violence, 74% had been beaten at least once while visibly pregnant. Although most of the men avoided hitting the women in the stomach, 16% of the men did aim blows at the woman's abdomen. In two of the cases the beatings were severe enough to have caused miscarriages.

Fighting Back. Fifty percent of the women reported that they had fought back physically at some time. In 40% of the above cases, fighting back only made the man angrier and more violent. In 36% of the cases it seemed to have had no effect whatsoever.

General Characteristics of Violent Couples

Relationship with Friends and Family. In 48% of the cases women reported that they had been forbidden by their husbands to have personal friends, or the husbands would not allow their wives' friends to come to the house. However, these men did have several of their own friends. Both husband and wife had several friends in 34% of the cases, 4% of the women said they had friends but their husbands did not, and in 7% of the couples neither partner had close friends. Fifty-six percent of the women reported that they and their husbands either "never" or only "rarely" went out together. Twenty-eight percent socialized "occasionally," and only 16% went out "often." Finally, in 78% of the cases, couples lived within close range of other family members. However, not all women were necessarily on good terms with either their in-laws or their own families.

Table 22

Why Beatings Stopped

	Percent of Cases
Never knew - he would suddenly stop and storm out	10
Never knew - he would suddenly stop	42
Agreed upon cue (woman gives in, faints, etc.)	16
Knew he would really harm her if he continued	8
Exhausted himself	2
She ran out of the house	10
She gave in	6
She left room	2

Verbal Abuse. Men subjected their wives to verbal abuse in 88% of the cases. Forty-two percent of the women reported having believed their husbands' negative evaluations. Furthermore, there was a positive correlation between the woman's believing this verbal abuse and her remaining for a relatively long time in the relationship ($r = +.42$, p less than .002).

Sexual Behavior. "Abnormal" sexual behavior in the men was reported in 34% of the cases. However, it should be noted that women were somewhat conservative in their evaluations of sexual activities. For example, many felt that oral sex was "kinky" and "sick." One man appeared to have been sadistic, requiring beatings for arousal, and one woman admitted that the abuse was sexually exciting. However, these two individuals were not married to each other.

Extramarital Activity. Twelve percent of the women said they had suspected their husbands of having had affairs. In 32% of the cases, the man had confirmed sexual liaisons at times throughout the entire marriage, while another 10% of the men had affairs only towards the end of the marriage when separation or divorce seemed imminent. Only 14% of the women said they had ever taken a lover, and even then, only towards the last of the marriage.

Length of Relationship. At the time of the interview, three of the women were still with their violent husbands, and had been married 21, 22, and 26 years respectively. In other cases, the marriages had lasted an average of 9.2 years. The range was 26 (see Table 23).

Years with Violence. Women stayed in a violent situation an average of 8.5 years. However, 24% lived with abuse from 11 to 20 years. The longest period recorded was a case in which the woman was still married, and had already spent

Table 23

Length of Relationship

Experimental Group

	Percent of Cases
1 - 3 years	18
4 - 9 years	38
10 - 15 years	28
17 - 20 years	10
21 or more years	6

26 years with violence (see Table 24).

Contact with Service Agencies

Ninety-six percent of the women in the Experimental Group had sought legal services at some time. Of that number, 59.6% reported having been moderately or completely satisfied with the services. However, the battered women were significantly less satisfied with their lawyers than were the non-battered women who had consulted an attorney (Chi Square = 6.88, df = 1, p less than .01).

Of the 39 "experimental" women who had had contact with the police because of the violence, 82.1% were either moderately or completely dissatisfied with the officers' response. Furthermore, women in the Control Group who had had occasion to call the police (e.g. to report a burglary or prowler) were significantly more satisfied with the service than were battered women (Chi Square = 8.99, df = 1, p less than .003).

Of the 44% of battered women who had seen a physician for treatment of injuries due to battering, 72.7% indicated that they had been pleased with the service. All of the "control" women reported satisfaction with their doctors' care (Chi Square = 9.39, df = 1, p less than .002).

Sixty-four percent of women in the Experimental Group and 35.9% of the women in the Control Group had at some time applied for financial aid from a Department of Public Social Services. Of that number, 76% of the battered women and 57% of the non-battered women indicated that they had not been satisfied with the agency's response (see Table 25).

Table 24

Number of Years With Violence

	Percent of Cases
Only one incident	8
1 - 6 months	2
6 months - 1 year	8
1 year	4
2 years	4
3 years	8
4 - 6 years	12
7 - 10 years	28
11 - 20 years	22
21 or more years	4

Table 25

Contact With Service Agencies

Experimental and Control Group Women

	No Contact	Complete Satisfaction	Moderate Satisfaction	Moderate Dissatisfaction	Complete Dissatisfaction
DPSS					
Experimental	25	1	5	10	9
Control	36	1	4	6	3
Pastor					
Experimental	20	9	9	7	5
Control	31	8	6	3	2
Psychiatrist					
Experimental	25	12	4	5	4
Control	44	0	5	0	1
Physician					
Experimental	28	11	6	4	1
Control	6	18	26	0	0
Police					
Experimental	12	8	6	6	18
Control	26	10	10	3	1
Lawyer					
Experimental	2	21	9	7	11
Control	19	15	13	2	1
Psychologist					
Experimental	20	17	7	5	1
Control	35	5	5	5	0
Social Worker					
Experimental	31	4	6	6	3
Control	41	2	4	2	1

Summary Analyses

Hypothesis Testing

A multiple regression analysis was performed in order to test the hypothesis that wife abuse would be best predicted by a combination of these factors: Violence in the background of both the man and woman, adherence to traditional sex-role models by both the man and woman, and the presence of situational stress. Since there was no direct measure of the man's traditionalism, dominance level was used as an indirect measure. It was not possible to obtain data on the woman's traditionalism during her marriage to a violent spouse. Situational stress was represented by three variables: job problems, financial difficulties, and man's extra-marital activity. Because comparable data on control couples was lacking for some of the above mentioned variables, it was not possible to use this multiple regression to predict the presence or absence of violence. Instead, a separate equation was derived for severity, frequency, and overall abuse. The number of years with violence was included because of its significant relationship with severity. However, this factor was deleted in the regression on abuse since duration had been used in computing the abuse score. Therefore, this regression used the following independent variables: Man's Dominance, Years with Violence, Violence in Man's Background, Did Couple Have Financial Problems?, Did Man Have Job Problems?, and Did Man Have Affairs?. All factors were entered stepwise.

The overall F scores for the multiple regressions on frequency and abuse were not significant. The overall F score for severity was significant ($F = 5.70$, (6, 43), p less than .01) with the formula accounting for 37% of the variance. The most important factors were Man'sDominance ($F = 15.76$, (1, 48), p less than .01), Years with Violence ($F = 5.31$, (2, 47), p less than .01), Violence in Man's Background (F = 4.76, (3, 46), p less than .01), and Did Couple Have Financial Problems: (F = 3.90, (4, 45), p less than .01). The remaining two variables taken individually or as a group did not add significantly to the predictive power of the equation. In fact, including these two factors actually reduced the amount of variance accounted for by the regression formula (see Table 26).

Characteristics of the Violence

In order to determine which combination of variables best predicted certain characteristics of the violence, a separate multiple regression equation was derived for severity, frequency, and overall abuse. Only those factors which already had been shown to be significantly related to the dependent variables were used in this analysis. The following variables were chosen: Man's Dominance, Violence in Man's Background, Violence in Woman's Background, Years with Violence, Status Inequality, Man's Education Level, and Man's Use of Alcohol. As before, the regression on overall abuse used all the above variables except Years with Violence. That factor was deleted because duration had been used in computing the abuse score. All factors were entered step-wise.

The overall F scores for the multiple regression on frequency and abuse were not significant. The overall F score of the regression on severity was significant (F = 4.24, (7.42), p less than .01), with the equation accounting for 32% of the total variance. The most important factors in predicting severity were Man's Dominance (F = 15.76, (1, 48), p less than .01), Years with Violence (F = 5.31, (2, 47), p less than .01), and Violence in Man's Background (F = 4.76, 3, 46), p less than .01). The remaining variables taken individually or as a

Table 26

Multiple Regression - Severity

Independent Variable	Simple R	Adjusted R Square	R Square Change	Beta
Man's Dominance	.497	.231	.247	.472
Years with Violence	.308	.295	.076	.306
Violence in Man's Background	.255	.347	.063	.262
Did Couple Have Financial Difficulties	.188	.386	.049	.182
Did Man Have Job Problems	.087	.377	.005	.085
Did Man Have Affairs	.111	.365	.002	.055

group did not significantly improve the predictive power of the regression. In fact, the inclusion of these factors actually reduced the amount of variance accounted for by the equation (see Table 27).

Prediction of Violence

In order to determine the power of certain variables to predict whether or not violence will occur, a discriminant analysis was performed. In this analysis independent variables were assigned the weights which provided the maximum discrimination between the Experimental and Control Groups. The following factors were used in the function: Violence in Woman's Background, Violence in Man's Background, Man's Use of Alcohol, and Status Inequality. Factors were chosen for inclusion only if they had been statistically significant in earlier comparison between groups. Man's Arrest Record was not considered to be an appropriate predictor variable because the category included men whose arrest had occurred within one year after the divorce.

The resulting canonical discriminant function was highly significant (Chi Square = 49.64, df = 5, p less than .00001). Although each of the variables made a statistically significant contribution to the overall function, Violence in Man's Background and Violence in Woman's Background were the two most important factors. Man's Education Level was the least important (see Table 28).

Qualitative Analyses

The Interview Situation

The discussion of both specific violent events and the

Table 27

Multiple Regression - Severity

Independent Variable	Simple R	Adjusted R Square	R Square Change	Beta
Man's Dominance	.497	.231	.247	.480
Years with Violence	.308	.295	.076	.256
Violence in Man's Background	.255	.347	.063	.257
Status Inequality	.032	.338	.005	-.187[a]
Violence in Woman's Background	-.176[b]	.324	.006	.104
Man's Education Level	.074	.333	.009	-.174[c]
Man's Use of Alcohol	.014	.317	.007	-.092[d]

a, b, c, d. Although these weights were not in the expected direction, their contributions were insignificant.

Table 28

Discriminant Function

Independent Variable	Standardized Canonical Coefficient	Univariate F Ratio	Significance[a] of F Ratio
Violence in Man's Family	-.67	.275	p .00001
Violence in Woman's Family	-.58	.137	p .0004
Woman's Education Level Compared to Man's	-.46	.146	p .0002
Man's Use of Alcohol	-.34	.541	p .02
Man's Education Level	-.01	.104	p .002

a. df = (1, 98)

abusive situation in general ordinarily elicited physiological reactions similar to those the woman experienced at the time of the actual beatings. For example, one developed a rash on her hands during the course of the interview. She reported that this rash had appeared before, and that her psychologist has felt that it was psychosomatic, caused by a repressed desire to strangle her husband. Other women indicated that their stomachs became "tied up in knots," and one woman told me that talking about past abuse brought back to her "the horrifying sound of flesh hitting flesh." Most women also showed signs of general anxiety, becoming tense, nervous, and "shaky" when describing violent incidents. Furthermore, these reactions occurred even when it had been many years since the battering had taken place.

In spite of the emotions and anxieties which the interview aroused, however, many women said that they had felt talking about the violence had been beneficial. It was not unusual for a woman to remark that she had gained new insight and had achieved a better understanding of the whole situation. It would appear that, although no actual counseling took place, the discussion of these events in an accepting, non-judgmental atmosphere was therapeutic.

Psychological State of the Women

The majority of the women seemed happy, stable, and self-confident at the time of the interview. In fact, many indicated they thought that their experiences with a violent spouse had made them strong. As one woman said, "I know that if I could get through that, I could get through *anything.*" Even women who had not received professional counseling reported that they had developed new feelings of self-worth, independence, and competence. Of course, not all women were this well-adjusted. For example, one of the respondents had just discovered that her third husband was violent, as were her first two. During the interview she repeatedly said that she knew that she deserved not to be beaten. However, my subjective impression was that she still did not have enough self-esteem or confidence to change the situation. I subsequently discovered that I had been correct; three months later she called a hot-line for battered women because her husband had just beaten her again.

Although most of the women seemed to be capable of dealing with their emotional reactions to the violence, few of them had been able to honestly confront their feelings about past mistreatment of their children. Intellectualization appeared to have been the most commonly used defense mechanism. A number of women could talk about incidents of physical and sexual abuse without displaying any emotion. For instance, one woman spoke at a very brisk rate throughout the interview, and could recount events of several years past in extraordinary detail. Neither her pace nor her emotional state changed in the slightest when she recounted at length how her husband had chronically abused their two children. My immediate reaction was that she could have just as easily been talking about the weather. It is interesting to note that the absence of affect occurred only in women who had never attempted to stop the mistreatment. By contrast, women who had successfully intervened at the first incident often became animated and angry when recounting the event.

Women varied considerably in the degree of their insight into the dynamics of the battering situation. Most women did seem to have achieved some understanding of their past interaction patterns. For example, several indicated that they felt their husbands needed to be protected and taken care of, and that responding to those needs was satisfying. Another women reported that she consciously and purposefully provoked the violent incidents in order to break the tension and to gain control over her subsequently contrite spouse. Finally, most respondents could cite specific reasons for their choice of a marriage partner, but few associated that choice with either childhood experiences or with their self-image at the time.

Possible Predisposing Factors

Family Background. Although the majority of men in this sample had not been exposed to violence as children, only two of the men had a good childhood. In all other cases there was either alcoholism, neglect, or an unhealthy relationship with one or both parents. For example, a number of women were of the opinion that their husbands had constantly tried to please their fathers but could never seem to quite satisfy paternal demands and expectations. By contrast, the mothers of several men had been extremely overprotective and indulgent. For instance, one woman said that her mother-in-law had kept her son like a "pet," refusing to allow him any normal interaction with other children. Many women also came from overprotective families, reporting that they had been raised as "little ladies," and that it had been improper to show any emotions, especially anger. Furthermore, these women had been given few freedoms or responsibilities as children. In fact, some respondents indicated that they didn't even know how to write a check at the time of their marriages.

Men's Personality Traits. Although the men in this sample were not characterized by any one personality "type," it is possible to identify some common traits. For example, many husbands evidently managed to keep rather tight control over most of their emotions; coworkers described them as "cool" and "unflappable," and wives reported that they rarely discussed feelings. These men were, however, quite able to express anger, both verbally and physically.

Many batterers also appear to have been very complex, often displaying contradictory traits and behavior. For example, one man had had a record of juvenile arrests due to violence, had been a boxer in the Marines, and had been quite severe in his verbal and physical abuse of his wife. However, this man was also a professional gardener who carefully nurtured beautiful flowers and patiently encouraged his sons in their own gardening efforts. Furthermore, although in general he rarely spoke to his wife, when he was out of town he would write her passionate love letters and telephone her every day.

Many women reported that their husbands' behavior and violence were almost totally unpredictable; some wives had absolutely no indication or warning that a beating was about to occur. For example, one woman described an incident in which her husband came home from work, greeted her in a friendly way, and gave her a kiss. In the course of their subsequent conversation, she asked him to take out the trash. Without a warning, he turned and punched her in the face. In addition, a number of men could make dramatic behavior changes in the midst of a beating. For instance, several women said that their husbands could be battering them severely, yet if a friend arrived unexpectedly these men would suddenly stop what they were doing and become quite calm, greeting the guests as if nothing unusual had been happening.

The majority of men in this sample were described as having been "jealous," and in many cases this jealousy appeared to have become pathological. For example, it was not uncommon for a husband to have a friend follow his wife to make sure that she went exactly where she said she was going to go. Two men put "taps" on the phone to record conversations, and one batterer actually timed how long it took his wife to get down to the laundry room and back to the house, telephoning her to make sure that she didn't do anything else in between her trips. Ordinarily, jealousy was sexual in nature, and men rarely confined their suspicions to any one particular person; women were usually accused of having affairs with several men, ranging from their bosses down to the milkman. In one case a woman said that they even had to stop having the paper delivered because her husband believed that she had taken the paperboy as her lover.

Characteristics of the Violence

"Non-Stereotype" Women (n - 4). These four respondents were labeled "non-Stereotype" because unlike the majority of women, they impressed me as having remained particularly strong-willed and self-confident throughout their marriages. All of them had retained decision-making power in important matters, and none of them made major changes in life-style to please their mates, or believed the content of their husband's verbal abuse. These women also mentioned that they never felt guilty about the beatings. Instead, they viewed the presence of abuse as primarily their husbands' fault.

"Non-stereotype" wives tended to spend a relatively short period of time in the abusive situation - two women stayed five years, one, two years, and one experienced only one incident of violence before leaving. Furthermore, one of the women who endured violence for five years experienced only "not severe" battering. In fact, the only two "not severe" cases of battering occurred in this subgroup. Although the "non-stereotype" women were not differentiated by education level or age married, none of the women described her family background as having been repressive, or said that she had been overprotected as a child. By contrast, 52% of the other women reported that their childhoods had been "repressive," and 56% said they had been "overprotected."

Finally, it would appear that the assertiveness these women displayed in their marriages also tended to generalize to other situations. For example, when one of these women found that the police response was inadequate, and that the district attorney was unwilling to press charges, she went directly to the mayor to complain about the poor service she had received.

Women Experiencing Only One Incident of Violence (n = 4). These four women were not differentiated from the rest of the sample by age married, education level, degree of childhood happiness, or by the woman's relationship with her mother. However, in three of these cases the husband had filed for divorce and only five men in the entire sample had initiated such proceedings. One can only speculate how long these women might have stayed if the men themselves had not wanted to separate. It is also interesting to note that in two of these cases there was a period of two years without physical abuse before the actual separation. In short, violence was not the immediate reason for the dissolution of these marriages.

Cases In Which Frequency and/or Severity of Violence Remained At the Same Level (n =10). The couples in this subgroup were not differentiated from the rest of the cases by violence in the background of either the man or woman, by status inequality, or by whether or not families had experienced financial difficulties. However, eight of the men had achieved only a high school education or less, and eight of the men were rated low in dominance. Seven of the husbands were described as being both "macho" and "jealous," but there were no other personality traits common to the majority of this subgroup.

Characteristics of the Marital Relationship

Emotional Abuse. Almost without exception, the women in this study reported that their husbands had subjected them to varying degrees of verbal abuse. Wives were told that they were incompetent, stupid, and incapable of surviving without masculine help and direction. Women were criticized for the way they wore their hair, the way they kept house, and the way they raised the children. Quite frequently a man's jealousy was the motivating factor in a verbal attack. For example, one woman mentioned that she could never seem to convince her husband that she had not been unfaithful to him, and that his suspicions led to constant abuse. As she said, "It wasn't until after I was divorced that I remembered that my given name was Kay. The whole time I was married I was always 'bitch' or 'whore' to my husband."

In many cases the verbal abuse also included blaming the woman for the violence. It was not unusual for a woman to be told that if she would, for example, stop flirting, cook better meals, or stop nagging, she would never be hit again. Furthermore, many women reported that they indeed felt that the beatings were their fault.

The effects of these verbal attacks should not be underestimated; every one of the women subjected to this kind of abuse maintained that the emotional mistreatment was far more devastating than any physical injuries they had suffered. As one woman said, "The bruises and cuts would always heal, but the emotional scars never did. I carried them with me all the time." The feelings of worthlessness induced by these verbal attacks were not only introjected by the women but also tended to generalize to other interpersonal relationships. In short, most battered women came to believe that other people also perceived them as unworthy and incompetent.

Cases In Which There Was Little or No Verbal Abuse (n = 6). These cases were not differentiated from the rest of the sample by severity, frequency, or duration of the violence. However, all of the men were rated high on dependency and low on dominance and hostility. Only one man was ever violent to other than family members. With regard to family background, three of the men had been exposed to violence as children, and four reportedly had had indulgent, overprotective mothers. Only two of the women had experienced violence in their families of origin. The degree of status inequality among couples in this subgroup was less than that found in the entire sample; only two women were better educated than their husbands.

It is also interesting to examine the women's perceptions of what their husbands were trying to accomplish by the violence. Even though all the men were listed as low in dominance, two of the women still felt that the violence had been used to achieve total control over them. However, in one such case there was only one incident before the woman left, and in the other, the woman was of the "non-stereotype" nature discussed earlier. Therefore, the men apparently did not achieve what they had expected from the beatings. Of the four remaining women, two never really knew why their husbands battered them, and two reported that the violence was always related to their husbands' desire for a specific sex act.

Relationships with Friends and Community Agencies. Many women in this study found that it had been easier to talk about the violence with a friend than with a family member. However, many women also reported that their friends usually said, "You're crazy to stay. You should get out." This reaction added to the woman's guilt about not having already left, and also reflected a lack of understanding of the complexity of the situation. Therefore, this kind of advice only tended to convince women that no one really knew what they were going through.

The response of family members varied greatly. Some parents refused to become involved in any way, while others provided their daughters with both financial and emotional support. A number of women were reluctant to reveal the abuse because of the genuine fear that their fathers would seek retribution by attacking their husbands.

Generally speaking, women who called the police were not totally satisfied with the response. Although some officers seemed interested and eager to help, many others appeared totally unconcerned about the woman's safety. In fact, one respondent said that she once overheard a policeman tell her husband, "I understand how it is. I have to put my wife in her place sometimes, too." In addition, it was not unusual for a woman to be told that the police would not come out because they had no jurisdiction in "domestic matters." Finally, most women who had obtained temporary restraining orders reported that these orders could not be enforced, and were of little value unless the man were on probation.

Finances. Families differed considerably with regard to how finances were handled. Some men let their wives control all the money, and never even knew the balance of checking or savings accounts. Other men decided how all the money was to be allocated, but then had the women, like secretaries, do all the paperwork. By contrast, several husbands had complete control over all the finances. In situations such as this, the man usually demanded that his wife turn over her paycheck to him, even if she were the sole or primary breadwinner.

Many men kept most of the money for themselves in order to buy liquor or indulge in hobbies or sports, often letting their wives and children do without necessities. One woman reported that at first she enjoyed the challenge of trying to feed the family on the $10.00 a week her spouse allowed her. However, her enjoyment did not last long. Several husbands were quite extravagant when buying items for themselves. Three of the men even went on manic-like spending sprees, with one man charging $3000.00 worth of clothes for himself in one afternoon. It would appear that the financial difficulties reported by several couples were not due to an insufficient level of income, but to the fact that budgets were "stretched" to accommodate the extravagant buying habits of the men.

Sexual Relationships. In general, the men in this sample appeared to have few sexual problems. However, a number of women did report that their husbands would sometimes force them to have relations, occasionally resorting to violence to obtain compliance. Many women said that they felt they had been raped by their husbands. By contrast, some men went for periods of as long as two years without having sexual intercourse with their wives. In addition, when one wife told her husband that she could not bear to have sexual relations with him right after a beating, he replied that he understood her feelings, and left her alone. In the majority of cases women reported that their desire for sexual intercourse diminished soon after the violence began, with only three women being able to maintain a good sexual relationship with their husbands for the duration of the marriage. There was but one case where the dominance and violence were sexually arousing to the woman, and she expressed considerable shame and guilt over those emotions.

Effects of the Violence

Effects on the Children. It was the rare child, indeed, who appeared to have escaped any ill effects from living in an atmosphere of violence. The majority of mothers reported that their youngsters exhibited some form of maladjustment or abnormal behavior. For example, many children suffered from psychosomatic illnesses such as asthma, or had difficulty sleeping, frequently awakening with nightmares. In a number of cases, children apparently began to take the violence as simply "a matter of course." For instance, one woman said that each time her husband started to hit her, her seven-year-old boy would take their four-year-old daughter by the hand and lead her out of the room. Another woman recalled that she finally decided to leave her husband when she found that her nine-year-old son was beating his six-year-old sister. The boy's explanation was, "If Daddy can do it, I can do it, too."

Several youngsters who witnessed the violence tried to intervene; they would scream, cry, pull on their mothers, or try to get in between the two combatants. The effect of these efforts was variable. Sometimes fathers would merely "brush them aside" or ignore them all together. However, in some cases men would stop battering, seemingly in response to their children's distress.

A number of children showed signs of severe disturbance. For instance, one four-year-old child completely stopped talking, and stayed wrapped in her mother's skirts whenever possible. In one family alone, three boys, aged sixteen to eighteen, still wet the bed, and the sixteen-year-old daughter sucked her thumb when distressed. Some of the women, but by no means the majority, had gotten counseling for their children. In fact, several women indicated they were well aware that a daughter had been sexually abused, or that their children had severe behavior disorders. However, professional help had never been sought for them. Furthermore, even when I suggested such a course of action would be advisable, some of these mothers still rejected the idea.

Long-Term Effects of Violence. As mentioned earlier, the majority of women who remarried chose non-violent second husbands. However, several women did say that, although they intended to marry again at some time, they felt they would never completely trust another man again. In addition, though most of the women could discuss the violence in a reasonably calm manner (physiological responses notwithstanding) a number of women said that they still had over-reacted to an implied physical threat from a man. For example, one woman described an incident in which her present, non-violent spouse had playfully put his hands at her neck. At this point she became hysterical, and started flailing wildly. She eventually ended up crouched in a corner, crying. This woman had not suffered any physical abuse for nine years. Clearly the effects of domestic violence are neither superficial nor necessarily transient in nature.

Post-Marriage Behavior. The majority of men in this study remarried after the divorce. Several of these second marriages, however, were unsuccessful, and a number of women had evidence that their ex-husbands also battered subsequent wives. Although two of the men did commit suicide, most of them did not "fall apart" once the relationship was ended. In fact, the psychological state of only two men seemed to deteriorate after the divorce. Furthermore, not all the men even made efforts to keep their wives from leaving. However, several women did report that after the divorce their ex-husbands found them and beat them, sometimes as part of a campaign to "win" them back, sometimes just to harass them.

Of the twenty-two women who had remarried, only two had chosen violent spouses the second time. In addition, many women reported that, despite past traumatic experiences with their first husbands, they had established loving, mutually satisfying relationships with their current spouses.

Woman's Reaction to the Violence. Almost without exception, women reported that both their feelings and their behavior toward their husbands changed over time. In cases where the violence was severe and/or of relatively long duration, women usually indicated that they first felt anger, then hatred for their husbands. Eventually, however, these emotions gave way to feelings of hopelessness and despair, with many such women describing themselves as "zombies." In couples where the violence was not quite as severe, women frequently indicated that they had gradually withdrawn emotionally from their husbands as a defense against the verbal abuse. These women said that the positive feelings they originally felt for their spouses were ultimately replaced by anger and fear.

Although one would expect that anger would be an almost universal response to abuse, nearly one half of the women did not include "anger" when describing their emotional reactions to the violence. Furthermore, even when anger was felt, it was rarely expressed directly. Considering the number of women who suffered from depression and psychosomatic illnesses, it would appear that the anger was frequently turned inward. However, some wives did find ways of passively aggressing. For example, one woman said that following a beating she would purposely serve her husband unappetizing foods. Other women would "forget" to do the laundry or waken their husbands in time for work.

Finally, it is interesting to note that many women said their husbands appeared to become incensed when verbal or physical abuse no longer seemed to have an effect on them. As one woman said, "When he (her husband) discovered he couldn't get at me anymore, he started in on the children. He knew *that* would get a reaction out of me."

Discussion

There are at least three limitations of the present research design which must be considered in evaluating results. First, all of the women who participated were volunteers who obviously felt comfortable about discussing personal, often painful experiences. Second, it is possible that there were strong demand characteristics associated with the interview situation. All of the respondents knew that the interviewer was the president of an organization which operated a hotline for battered women. Therefore, women might have tried to appear independent and "liberated." The desire to present such an image might have been intensified in cases where women had remarried, since they would want it to appear that they had learned something from their first marriages. Finally, with the exception of three cases, data were retrospective in nature, and one would anticipate that certain errors of memory would have occurred. This problem may be particularly troublesome in studies of wife abuse since almost all women reported that they tended to "block out" memories of their experiences with violence. In addition, all information about the husbands was "second hand." Therefore, it is possible that a woman's feelings of animosity, or simply the limitations of her perceptiveness could have influenced accounts of her husband and his behavior.

Characteristics of the Violence - Frequency, Severity, and Duration

Hypotheses. Results from the current study do not confirm the hypothesis that men who experience financial difficulties, job problems, or chronic unemployment will be more severe and/or frequent in their violence than men who are economically and occupationally secure. However, even in cases where the income was sufficient, beatings may have been precipitated by arguments over how the money was to be spent. Since many batterers reportedly had extravagant and selfish buying habits, one might expect that the disbursement of income would be a source of contention. Therefore, it is possible that disagreements over finances rather than the lack of money per se may be related to the severity and/or frequency of wife abuse.

Although the hypothesis could not be tested directly, there is some evidence to suggest that men who adhere to a traditional sex-role model are more violent than men who are less rigid. It could be argued that dominance over women is one aspect of the stereotyped masculine image. Results indicated that there was a positive correlation between a man's level of dominance and the severity of his physical abuse. Furthermore, there was a negative relationship between severity and the man's dependency, a trait not associated with the traditional male role.

When attempting to predict the presence or absence of wife abuse, however, there is at least one reason that this result should be interpreted with caution. In the present study there was also a positive correlation between dominance and hostility. Without comparable measures for a control population, it cannot be determined whether the high severity was due to traditionalism alone or caused by the combination of traditionalism and hostility. In short, it is quite possible that there are men who adhere to a stereotyped role model but are not violent.

Although the hypothesis could not be tested directly, results do suggest that women tend to endure more years of violence if they adhere to a traditional sex-role model or if they have relatively low self-esteem. With regard to the latter, one could assume that wives who reported believing their husbands' verbal abuse had lower self-esteem than wives who did not accept their spouses' negative evaluations. The positive correlation between believing the abuse and duration of the violence therefore provides partial support for that hypothesis.

Although it was not possible to obtain a measure of a woman's traditionalism at the time of the marriage, both Catholicism and Mormonism are associated with conservative values. Furthermore, women who belonged to those churches did stay with a violent man longer than women of other religious affiliations. However, adherence to traditional sex-role models is certainly not confined to any particular religion or sect. Therefore, this finding is only suggestive of the relative importance of a woman's traditionalism in determining the duration of domestic violence.

Typologies of Violence. Although it was not possible to identify categorically different types of violence on the basis of severity, frequency, and duration, results indicate that the perceived motivation for the violence may be a useful means of categorizing the physical abuse. More precisely, there were differences between violence which was used for specific purposes, such as winning an argument, and violence which was related to the man's desire to obtain control over most, if not all, of his wife's behavior.

In the latter category, the abuse was not only more

severe, but was also associated with higher degrees of hostility and overall alcohol use by the man. In addition, husbands who were perceived as using aggression to gain total control and dominance over their wives tended to be violent to individuals outside the immediate family. Furthermore, in all cases where violence had a limited objective, women said that they had been able to end a beating by giving a certain "cue." In short, it would appear that once these men had achieved their goals in any given situation they stopped their attacks. By contrast, women who felt that their husbands wanted complete domination were never able to stop the battering by giving a "cue." Finally, there was a negative correlation between a man's using violence for domination and his experiencing job problems. Therefore, one could speculate that this type of abuse may be primarily related to the assailant's personality traits rather than to external stresses.

If the man's motivation does differentiate types of domestic violence, it may be appropriate to develop a variety of different treatment programs for batterers. For example, men who use force in specific instances might not require long-term psychotherapy, but might only need to learn new methods for coping with frustration. Since abusive men are notorious for their resistance to traditional therapy, the proper selection of clients and treatment could improve the "cure rate" for wife abuse.

Comparison with Other Forms of Aggression. In order to understand the nature of domestic violence, it is necessary to specify which aspects are associated with aggression in general and which are peculiar to the marital relationship. With regard to the former, wife abuse shares at least two characteristics in common with the aggressive behavior observed in laboratory settings. First, a number of studies have found that aggression tends to escalate over time. For example, several experiments have been conducted in which participants administered shocks to "learners" in order to help them master certain material. Results showed that subjects generally increased the intensity of the shocks over the trials (Goldstein, Davis, & Herman, 1975). A similar, more recent study used feedback in the form of verbal phrases of varying aversiveness. It was found that subjects escalated negative feedback regardless of the learner's performance (Benton & Wichman, Note 20).

The authors suggested that the thoery of disinhibition of anti and prosocial behaviors most adequately accounts for the results. More specifically, it is assumed that in almost any given situation norms exist for both the inhibition and expression of the behavior. A person's decision to act will depend upon the number and relative importance of these competing norms. However, once the behavior has been performed, norms which sanction its display become more salient, while any inhibitory norms become less cogent. This, in turn, reduces the conflict, making further occurrences of the act even more likely. In the case of aggression, disinhibition may also be facilitated by the fact that the reduction in blood pressure and arousal which follows an outburst is assumed to be positively reinforcing: "The two interacting processes - ever increasing inherent pleasure in the aggressive response and the reduced inhibitions accompanying the response - result in escalation" (Benton & Wichman, Note 21, p. 23).

The theory of disinhibition also provides a plausible explanation for the violence that occurs in domestic situations. As mentioned earlier, although there are no longer formal norms which sanction wife abuse, there still exists a well-established tradition which gives a husband the right to batter his wife. Furthermore, it is reasonable to assume that norms sanctioning wife abuse would be more salient for men who had observed violence as children than for men from non-violent families. Therefore, this theory could also account for the fact that abuse was relatively more severe among husbands from violent backgrounds.

Second, in laboratory studies it is quite common for an aggressor to devalue his victim. More specifically, the victim is condemned for bringing the abuse upon himself because of his behavior or faulty character. The perpetrator is therefore able to avoid taking full responsiblity for his violence. For example, in one learning experiment there was a significant difference between subjects' evaluations of their partners based on the type of feedback administered; subjects who had given aversive verbal feedback consistently rated their partners as having been uncooperative, unlikeable and unintelligent, while participants who had given positive feedback rated their partners more favorably (Benton & Wichman, Note 22). When devaluation continues over time, the victims frequently come to believe the verbal abuse themselves. Bandura has described the process this way: "Negative attribution by itself may not be too persuasive, but it is usually accompanied by maltreatment that produces self-confirming evidence of the victim's defects or badness. Vindicated inhumanity is thus more likely to instill self-contempt in victims than if it does not justify itself" (Bandura, 1973, p. 214). With regard to the present study, devaluation of the victim was almost universal, with over half of the women indicating that they had introjected their husbands' negative assessments. Therefore, domestic violence is in some ways similar to other aggressive behavior.

However, there are several reasons why wife abuse may represent a special case of aggression. First, since the assailant and victim are involved in an ongoing relationship, the battering takes place in a situation characterized by high levels of interaction. Furthermore, this factor could theoretically intensify the abuse. For example, it would not be feasible to control the aggression by limiting the sheer amount of contact between the two parties. In addition, any act of violence will necessarily influence the quality of the entire relationship; incidents of battering are part of an enduring process, not isolated events. It is therefore possible that the beatings and subsequent reactions could form a feedback system of ever increasing violence.

Finally, because of its ongoing nature, domestic violence is associated with at least two variables which do not ordinarily affect other forms of aggressive behavior. First, the very act of avoiding abuse by leaving the situation necessarily involves negative consequences for the woman. For example, over half the women in the present study indicated that financial considerations influenced their decision to remain in the marriage. It is also worth noting that the majority of women who had tried to obtain financial aid from public sources had been dissatisfied with the service they received. In short, the woman who lacked personal resources apparently found few alternatives to remaining with her violent husband if she were to preserve her economic security. In addition, social factors may influence the duration of the relationship; women who belonged to religions in which marriage was highly valued, and divorce, unacceptable, did indeed have longer marriages than women whose religious beliefs were less tradition.

Second, the very context of wife abuse provides rewards not present in other violent interactions. More specifically, results indicate that women received intermittent, positive reinforcement from their husbands. For example, in some cases, men made an effort to be nice to their wives after a beating, doing their best to please them in whatever way they could. A few women even reported that they were consciously aware of the power and control they enjoyed by manipulating their husbands' guilt over the violence. In addition, many women may have unconsciously used their husbands' temporary cooperativeness as a means of getting what they wanted. Second, in cases where women said their husbands were capable of being sweet and charming, women tended to stay married for relatively long periods. Presumably, these men were providing some rewards, if only intermittently. By contrast, women who described their husbands as "cold" tended to spend less time in the marriage. Finally, many women reported that their husbands had made an effort to keep them from leaving, telling them how much they were loved, how important it was to keep the marriage together. Some men even expressed extreme remorse after a beating.

It is also possible that women may have remained in the violent relationship because it allowed them to assume a nurturing, protective role. In fact, the single most common reason given by wives for staying was that they felt sorry for their husbands and wanted to help them. The opportunity to satisfy such a need would not only provide positive reinforcement in the interaction, but would also represent a negative consequence of leaving; women would not want to abandon a loved one. Indeed, many respondents mentioned that they had felt slightly guilty about leaving men who said they would be "lost" without them.

It also appears that several variables which ordinarily inhibit aggression may not reduce the level of domestic violence. For example, some laboratory experiments have found that guilt and self-criticism tend to reduce aggression (Baron, 1971; Buss, 1966). In the present study, however, men who displayed guilt and remorse were no less violent than men who did not express such emotions. In addition, it has been suggested that boys are more likely to be punished for aggression against girls than against other boys, and that these socialization experiences would later inhibit their aggression toward women. However, although this hypothesis has been confirmed by some research (Taylor & Epstein, 1967), several husbands in the present sample were extremely violent to their wives. Furthermore, the majority of men were not aggressive toward other adult males, confining their abuse to a single female target. Finally, neither the presence of witnesses or police, nor the visible pregnancy of the woman significantly lowered the level of the abuse.

Perhaps the most parsimonious explanation for the failure of these variables to reduce domestic violence is that certain social conditions tended to outweigh most potentially inhibiting effects. For example, although the police intervened in several cases, only two men were ever actually prosecuted for wifebeating. In addition, even when witnesses were present, they rarely interceded on the part of the woman. In short, almost none of the men ever had to suffer social disapproval for their behavior. In fact, as mentioned earlier, informal sanctions for wife abuse are still quite prevalent in our society. Therefore, batterers ordinarily avoid most of the aversive consequences ordinarily associated with aggression.

Predisposing Factors

Hypotheses. Results confirm earlier findings (Carlson, 1977; Gayford, 1975; Roy, 1977) in supporting the hypothesis that childhood exposure to violence is strongly associated with wife abuse. In the current study, the presence of violence in the family of origin discriminated between the Experimental and Control Groups and batterers who had experienced violence as children were later relatively more severe in the physical abuse of their spouses. The theory best able to account for the importance of childhood violence is Bandura's (1973) Social Learning Theory. According to

Bandura, aggression is a learned response transmitted primarily through the process of modeling. In a series of laboratory studies with children, it was found that exposure to aggressive models not only reduced the subjects' inhibitions against performing such acts, but also taught them new ways of aggressing. Furthermore, imitation was facilitated when the model was either rewarded or suffered no adverse consequences because of his behavior. Children were also more likely to imitate a model of higher status rather than one of low status (Bandura, 1973). Although there is presently no empirical evidence to suggest that aggressive responses learned through social observation are retained over long periods of time, there are several similarities between Bandura's experimental studies and the childhood experiences of many batterers. To begin with, a man who observed his own father beating his mother has been exposed to a model with relatively high status. Furthermore, if the woman had never taken any action against her husband, it is reasonable to assume that the children would learn that certain types of aggression could be performed with relative impunity. In addition, it has been suggested that children who are physically abused tend to associate love with physical aggression (Straus, 1978). In such cases, it would be more likely that both men and women who had been abused as children would have a tendency to view battering as normative behavior.

It is somewhat more difficult to determine how the experience of viewing wife abuse later affected the battered woman. Although she could not have identified directly with the model, she could have been socialized to view domestic violence as normal. However, since women in the present sample who had been exposed to childhood violence did not stay longer with an abusive man or endure more severe violence than women from non-violent families, it is likely that the effects of such experiences are indirect. Insight into the possible operation of these factors may be gained by examining the effects of violence on the children of the battered women in the current study. The majority of these youngsters had emotional problems, and it is not unreasonable to assume that any child growing up in an atmosphere of abuse would have difficulty developing a good self-image. This lack of self-esteem would no doubt later be reflected in the choice of a husband. In addition, the women in the present sample would have suffered the unmitigated effects of such experiences; none of the respondents who had been sexually or physically abused or had observed violence reported ever having had psychological counseling as children or adolescents. Therefore, results suggest that violence in the families of origin of both the man and the woman is correlated with later abuse.

In spite of the importance of background violence, however, it must be noted that more than half of the men who became batterers and over half of the women who became abused had reportedly experienced no violence as children. Therefore, it is necessary to also consider other elements in the family background which might be associated with subsequent aggression. Although the data do not allow for a precise analysis, it is possible to tentatively identify certain of these factors. First, the majority of women reported having had an unsatisfactory relationship with their mothers. In addition, many respondents indicated that they had not had good communication with their parents. Women who reported having been raised strictly also tended to spend a relatively long period of time in a violent marriage, while "non-stereotype" women indicated that their parents had been neither overprotective nor repressive. It is therefore possible that the presence of parental over-control resulted in feelings of low self-esteem and/or lack of self-confidence.

Most of the men in this sample also reportedly did not

have good interaction with their parents. The majority of men had at some time expressed either dislike or hatred for their mothers, and parental neglect or exceedingly high expectations were sometimes present. It is possible that elements of a man's childhood experience resulted in feelings of inadequacy and insecurity which later resulted in intense jealousy, the need to dominate, and the use of violence to assert himself and reestablish feelings of self-worth. By contrast, men who were reportedly overprotected by their mothers were less severe in their violence than men who had not had indulgent mothers. Although there was no statistical relationship between having had an overprotective mother and later dependency scores, it is possible that some men might have transferred maternal dependency to their wives.

Education Level. As has been found in other studies (Parker & Schumaker, 1977), there was a significant difference between violent and non-violent men with regard to education level. However, there are two reasons why results from the present study do not conclusively demonstrate that wife abuse is necessarily more prevalent among less educated men. First, when other variables, such as background violence, were analyzed together, education level was a relatively unimportant factor in discriminating between the Experimental and Control Groups. Second, since the women in this sample tended to marry men less educated than themselves, it is not clear whether or not the violence was actually due to the relatively lower education levels of the men, or to some other factor, such as the education levels of the men, or to some other factor, such as the stress created when a woman is more educated than her husband. Although status inequality was not a statistically significant variable, the relationship between education level and violence would still be more easily interpretable among couples where the man and the woman were of equal educational status.

Personality Traits. Because measures of personality were obtained after the battering had occurred, it is not possible to infer causality between personality traits and violence. However, it is possible to identify some of the relationships between certain personality factors and the physical abuse. To begin with, although other researchers (Martin, 1976; Walker, 1979) have suggested that violence occurs because of a conflict between the man's dependency and dominance needs, this hypothesis was not supported by the present study. In fact, high dominance was negatively correlated with some behaviors associated with dependency, such as the man's attempt to convince his wife not to leave. In addition, dependent men were not highly hostile as might be expected if they were experiencing the kind of conflict described above. In fact, the men who were not verbally abusive were all rated "high" on dependency. Finally, the men who were rated as being relatively more dependent upon their wives were less violent than men who were rated "low."

Results from the current study also provide a profile of the man who is relatively more severe in his violence. Men who tended to be more violent towards their wives were usually described as being jealous and insecure[23], experienced violence as children, were generally high in expressed hostility towards their spouses, did not appear to have strong dependency needs, and were rated "high" in behaviors perceived to be used for the purpose of total domination.

Although other authors (Davidson, 1978) have suggested a typology of personality based on the generality of the man's violence, men in this study who were violent to others were not significantly less remorseful than men who confined their abuse to family members. In other words, the dichotomy between men who were violent to others and not remorseful about their abuse and men who were violent only to family members and expressed considerable guilt over their aggressive behavior, was not found.

Although this study did not employ a direct measure of the traditionalism of the man, one might assume that the efforts to be dominating were reflective of adherence to a rather rigid, stereotyped male role. However, dominance over the woman is but one part of a total constellation of traits and behaviors associated with traditionalism. Therefore, results pertaining to traditionalism in the men can only be viewed as speculative. With regard to the women, although the battered wives did have less traditional attitudes toward the marital relationship than did the non-battered women, it must be remembered that all but three scores were obtained after the violent marriages had been terminated. It is likely that women who had formerly been in a violent relationship had subsequently changed their attitudes about marriage, particularly if they were currently married to a non-violent spouse. Furthermore, it is possible that demand characteristics influenced their responses. In short, this result does not necessarily indicate that battered women are less traditional in their attitudes than non-battered women.

Finally, since it was impossible to directly assess the personality traits of the women at the time of their marriages, one can only speculate as to the characteristics present at that time. However, based on self-reports of the women and on information about childhood experiences and later reactions to emotional abuse, it is reasonable to conclude that the majority of women who became battered wives were relatively low in self-esteem at the time of the marriage. This low self-esteem was reflected in the overall choice by women of men from lower educational and sometimes lower socioeconomic groups. A poor self-image or low self-esteem would also facilitate the introjection of the emotional abuse, and attribution to the woman of the guilt and responsibility for the violence in their relationship. Furthermore, it would be anticipated that those women who described their childhoods as overprotective and repressive would necessarily be less self-confident, independent and autonomous. However, beyond these conclusions, it is not possible to specify what, if any, personality characteristics are common to women who eventually become battered.

Factors Surrounding the First Violent Incident

Without exception, the first violent incident was either associated with some type of situational stress or was preceded by a verbal argument. This finding suggests that the very first use of violence may have been a response to frustration. In addition, many women felt that the first use of violence had "broken the ice," and that their husbands seemed to find it successively easier to resort to physical force. Apparently, the initial incident served to disinhibit the men's prohibitions against aggression. It is also interesting to note that although the first episode of violence appeared to reflect a classic frustration-aggression paradigm, in many instances the abuse later generalized to situations in which stress was less evident; many women perceived that their husbands later used violence as a means of achieving total domination and control over them.

Possible Facilitating Factors

It is somewhat difficult to assess the role of stress in precipitating or maintaining violence; data were not detailed enough to allow for the correlation of events external to the marriage with specific beatings, increases in frequency, or increases in severity. However, it is possible to identify in general those stresses which might have been present. To begin with, violent and non-violent couples were not differentiated by age married or number of children. Therefore, the abuse could not be primarily attributed to either the immaturity of the man and woman or to economic deprivation because of family size. In fact, many violent marriages were quite financially secure. Of course, it is possible that other than financial stresses could have been present. For example, a number of women reported that their husbands had had affairs. This infidelity might have produced guilt feelings or frustration which later led to beatings.

It is also somewhat difficult to assess the relative importance of the fact that violent men had had significantly more arrests than non-violent men. Since most arrests were caused by drunkenness rather than being crimes of robbery or assault, it is unlikely that this statistic is reflective of a criminal subculture. Rather, the high level of alcoholism among batterers and arrests related to inebriation might be indicative of a certain degree of stress which the men could not handle. Therefore, it is not possible to conclusively determine the type and importance of situational stresses among the violent couples in this study.

Comparison with Other Studies

Demographics. The current study confirmed the finding of Parker & Schumaker (1977, p. 761) that violent men were generally less educated than non-violent men. In addition, the frequency distribution of education levels for men was similar to that reported by Carlson (1977, p. 456). However, the women in the above study were less educated and less likely to have been employed than the women in the present research. In addition, when compared to this study, nearly three times as many men were chronically unemployed, and only half as many were professionals or managers

(Carlson, 1977, p. 456).

Although the present study found no significant relationship between a man's education level and the later degree of violence, Gelles (1972) found an inverse relationship in education level and degree of abuse. Finally, the present study confirmed O'Brien's (1971) finding that, in general, violent men were on average less educated than their wives.

Characteristics of the Violence. The present study differed considerably from Gelles (1972) work with regard to whether or not the violence was witnessed by other than immediate family members. None of Gelles' respondents were ever beaten in the presence of anyone but a family member, while 40% of the women in the current study said that the battering had been witnessed either by a neighbor, a friend, or a combination of a family member and a friend or neighbor.

There was also a disparity between the current research and other studies with regard to child abuse. Although over half the men in Gayford's (1975, p. 196) study and 33% of the men in Walker's (1979, p. 27) study had been child abusers, only 16% of the husbands in the present sample were reported to have been chronic child abusers. It is possible, of course, that other researchers had subsumed cases where there was only one incident of abuse under "child abuse." If single-incident cases are included in this category, then 28% of the men in the present research engaged in abuse at least once.

Reaction to the Violence. The present study confirmed Roy's (1978) finding that women stayed in a violent situation primarily because they felt sorry for their husbands and hoped their spouses would eventually reform. In addition, in Roy's (1978, p. 31) study women ranked "economics" fifth in importance out of seven possible reasons for staying, a rating comparable to that given by the respondents in the current sample. The present research did not, however, confirm Walker's (1979) finding that all violent men are remorseful after a beating. Furthermore, although some researchers (Hilberman & Munson, 1977; Walker, 1979) have reported that the psychological state of many batterers tend to deteriorate after divorce, the majority of men in this study did not appear to suffer any particular ill effects from the separation, many of them remarrying within a short length of time.

Social Factors. In the present study the incidence of violence in the batterer's background was below that reported in other research (Carlson, 1977, p. 456; Gayford, 1975, p. 195; Roy, 1977, p. 30). The number of women in this sample who experienced violence in their families of origin was similar to the percentages noted in some studies (Carlson, 1977, p. 456; Gayford, 1975, p. 195; Roy, 1977, p. 30), but below that found by Hilberman & Munson (1978) and Parker & Schumaker (1977). However, some of the percentages in other studies were confounded with other variables. Finally, in contrast to the Carlson study (1977), the women in the present sample who had been exposed to childhood violence did not tend to stay longer in a violent relationship than women whose backgrounds were non-violent (see Table 29).

Personality Factors. Results from the present study confirm other research which characterized the batterer as jealous (Hilberman & Munson, 1978; Martin, 1976; Scott, 1974; Walker, 1979), insecure (Martin, 1976; Walker, 1979), and moody (Martin, 1976). However, some findings are in contradiction with other studies. First, only about one quarter of the men were described as having had two different personalities. Walker (1979) and Davidson (1978) had previously reported that this duality was a common trait among violent men. Second, some researchers have suggested that

Table 29

Comparison With Other Studies

Violence[a] In Man's Background

Gayford N=100 (1975)	Carlson N=101 (1977)	Roy N=150 (1977)	Present Study N=50
51%	50%	81.1%	44%

Violence[a] In Woman's Background

Hilberman & Munson N=60 (1978)	Gayford N=100 (1975)	Carlson N=101 (1977)	Parker & Schumaker N=20 (1977)
50%[b]	23%	33%	90%

Roy N=150 (1977)	Present Study N=50
33.3%	33%

a. Wife abuse and/or child abuse
b. Confounded with paternal alcoholism

the abusive man experienced extreme conflict over his feelings of dependency on his wife and his need to be dominant (Davidson, 1978; Hilberman & Munson, 1978; Martin, 1976; Walker, 1979). However, in the current study there was a negative correlation between reported dominance and certain behaviors which reflected dependency. In addition, higher levels of dependency were associated with lower overall abuse.

The majority of women in the present sample appear to have had low self-esteem at the time of their marriages, a finding consistent with other research (Carlson, 1977; Roy, 1978; Walker, 1979). Although it was not possible to obtain a direct measure of a woman's self-image, it is unlikely that women with high self-esteem would marry men who were both less educated and from lower socio-economic levels than they. Furthermore, half of the women reported that they came to believe the content of their husbands' verbal abuse.

The number of alcoholic men in the present study was far below that reported by Carlson (1977, p. 457), Gelles (1972, p. 111), or Roy (1977, p. 39). In addition, the men in this sample were much less likely to have been drunk when violent than men in earlier studies (Carlson, 1977, p. 457; Gelles, 1972, p. 111; Roy, 1977, p. 39). Furthermore, although Roy (1977) and Walker (1979) found that alcoholic men were more frequent and severe in their violence, the level of alcohol use was not related to violence in the present study. Finally, the number of men in the present sample who had been arrested at least once was somewhat higher than rates reported by either Carlson (1977, p. 457) or Gayford (1975, p. 196) (see Table 30).

Relationship with Family and Other Agencies. As found in Walker's study (1979) the majority of women in this sample were not isolated from family members. How-

Table 30

Comparison With Other Studies

Alcoholism Rate Among Batterers

Gayford[a] N=100 (1975)	Hilberman & Munson N=60 (1978)	Roy N=150 (1977)	Present Study N=50
52%	97%	90%[b]	38%

Husband Arrested At Least Once

Carlson N=73 (1977)	Gayford N=100 (1975)	Present Study N=50
44%	52%	67%

Husband Always Drunk When Violent

Carlson N=101 (1977)	Gelles N=40 (1972)	Roy N=150 (1977)	Present Study N=50
60%	48%	More than 80%[c]	20%

a. Reported as "frequently drunk"
b. In relationships of seven years or more duration
c. Of the men who drank occasionally

ever, as reported by Hilberman & Munson (1978) and Carlson (1977), many men prevented their wives from having close friends. With regard to police involvement, the number of women in the current sample who called the police was slightly below that in Roy's (1978, p. 36) research, but far above the number in Walker's (1979) research. In addition, 70% of the women in Roy's study felt that the police had been unhelpful, while 63% of the women in the current sample who had called the police had been either moderately or completely dissatisfied with the response.

Implications of Comparisons Among Studies. When findings from the current study are integrated with earlier research there is evidence that most variables associated with wife abuse are apparently more complex than previously reported. For example, it appears that there is no one personality profile of the batterer. Both dependent men and dominant men may be violent. Men who are friendly and warm to other people, and men who are cold, withdrawn, and aloof abuse their wives. Men also differed considerably with regard to the degree of remorse they felt; although some men seem to be extremely sorry and guilt-ridden because of their aggression, many do not ever even apologize for their behavior. In addition, couples who have financial problems experience violence, but so do couples who are economically secure. Wife abuse can be unwitnessed or occur in the presence of others. Men who drink heavily abuse their wives, but so do men who never drink at all. Finally, batterers and their victims come from both violent and non-violent backgrounds. Therefore, it may not be possible to identify any one variable or pattern common to all cases of domestic violence.

Relationship of Results to Theories of Domestic Violence

The present research also did not support Walker's

theory of violence. The majority of couples did not experience a cycle consisting of the three phases she postulated - a tension-building stage, a major violent episode, and a period of relative calm. Furthermore, most of the men were not particularly remorseful after a beating. Finally, although most women displayed some symptoms of learned helplessness such as depression and indecisiveness, in many cases a first attempt to leave the violent situation was successful. In other words, not all women required the rehearsal of behaviors as predicted by Walker.

Findings from the current study do not confirm Gelles' (1972) theory that wifebeating is more prevalent among lower socio-economic groups. There was no significant different between the occupation levels of violent and non-violent men. Furthermore, although violent men had lower education levels than non-violent men, there are two reasons this finding does not imply that wife abuse is more prevalent in low socio-economic groups. First, there was no significant difference between Experimental and Control Groups on man's occupation. Second, since the majority of battered women had been employed during the marriage, their combined incomes could have placed them at economic levels above those indicated by the man's job alone.

Results also did not support Gelles' proposition that childhood exposure to violence is a necessary factor in wife abuse; over one half of the men in the present sample reportedly came from non-violent homes and presumably would not have been socialized to view aggression as an appropriate response to anger or frustration. In fact, it is doubtful that theories based on only one or two predisposing variables will ever be able to reliably predict whether or not violence will occur in any given relationship.

Findings from the current study suggest that there may

be a "lethal combination" of factors which are predisposing to domestic violence. More specifically, results of the discriminant analysis indicate that wife abuse is most likely to occur in couples where both the man and woman experienced violence in their families of origin, and the woman is better educated than her husband, and the man is a relatively heavy drinker. It is further proposed that some type of situational stress or frustration, however minor, is necessary to precipitate the first incident. Once the initial beating has taken place, however, situational variables are relatively less important than the man's personality traits, social factors (i.e. violence in man's background) and duration of the relationship in determining the severity of the subsequent abuse. Men who experienced violence as children and/or were rated "high" in domination were more severe in their battering than men who were from non-violent backgrounds and/or were rated "low" in domination. There was also a positive correlation between severity and duration.

It is important to note, however, that the above theory has two limitations. First, the effects of status inequality may not necessarily be due to the discrepancy in education levels per se. It is feasible that the actual predisposing factor is low self-esteem in the woman which has been reflected in her choice of a man less educated than she. Second, it is not possible to accurately assess the relative importance of certain personality traits among batterers. It has already been demonstrated that a man's degree of dominance is related to the severity of the physical abuse. It is quite probable that this characteristic is also present before the beatings begin and predisposes the man to use violence against his wife. These issues will need to be clarified by future research.

Suggestions for Future Research

Results of the present study suggest that there are a number of issues which should be investigated more fully. To begin with, since so few studies have used control groups, it is necessary to compare violent and non-violent couples on several variables. First, information is needed regarding the character and quality of childhood experiences. For example, the quality of the interaction between the subjects and their parents could be examined. It might also be interesting to examine parental attitudes toward appropriate masculine and feminine roles.

Second, it would be valuable to investigate the number and degree of situational stresses that couples experienced. Such information would make it possible to determine whether or not batterers tend to be inadequate in other areas of their lives, such as in their jobs. If the stresses are about equal for both groups, it would suggest that either abusive men are less able to handle stress or that domestic violence is primarily precipitated by factors other than frustration.

Third, studies should focus on the pre-battering stage of violent relationships. The data could then be compared to a similar period in non-violent couples, thereby providing a means of identifying patterns of interaction which are associated with subsequent physical abuse.

Fourth, future research should be directed toward specifying both situational variables and events within the relationship which are correlated with increases in the frequency and severity of violence. It is not yet possible to determine whether these increases are due to circumstances peculiar to the domestic situation or whether they are simply characteristics of aggression in general. If escalation of the violence in wife abuse is associated with unique factors, knowledge of such variables could facilitate development of treatment programs.

Finally, research has indicated that wifebeating is a wide-spread and highly complex phenomenon. In fact, it may never be possible to identify any one factor or combination of factors present in all cases of domestic violence. Therefore, it may be worthwhile to study marriages where there is no violence. If successful couples share common characteristics which differentiate them from violent families, the specification of these variables would allow for both the development of more effective therapy, and for the establishment of programs designed to prevent the occurrence of wife abuse.

Implications for Public Policy

Results from the present study indicate that community response to the needs of battered women is generally inadequate. First, although private psychologists and psychiatrists were frequently contacted, relatively few women ever saw a social worker. Although participants were not asked to explain why they did or did not have dealings with an agency, there is evidence that women may simply not have known that the Department of Public Social Services offers counseling; phone workers on a hot line for battered women often report that callers are almost totally unaware of public resources (Hofeller). This situation could no doubt be improved by better publicity, particularly through the media.

Second, in both the Experimental and Control Groups the majority of women who had applied for financial aid from the welfare department were not satisfied with the help they received. The most frequent complaints were that bureaucratic "red tape" created frustrating delays, and the workers sometimes seemed unsympathetic and insensitive.

Although there may not be enough county money to reduce the case load or provide better training for eligibility workers, some effort should be made to simplify the processes involved in obtaining cash grants. It ordinarily takes a day or two for funds to arrive, and having to wait for even a short period of time can sometimes be a genuine hardship for a battered woman. In many cases a woman must leave her house in a hurry, having no time to gather documents or money. If there is no place for her to stay without expense, she must either return to a potentially dangerous situation, or spend the night on the streets. One respondent in the current study mentioned that she often parked her car in a lot and slept there.

A possible solution to this problem might be to establish a special program providing immediate funds for temporary shelter in life threatening situations. Ideally, this program would be coordinated with other agencies experienced in delivering services to battered women. Clients would therefore also receive necessary counseling, information, and referral. Theoretically, of course, there are any number of churches and organizations which could initiate and support such a project. However, since the community response has generally been inadequate, the Department of Public Social Services may be the only practical resource, at least in the immediate future.

Third, many more battered women than non-battered women reported being dissatisfied with police intervention. The degree of frustration and discouragement with law enforcement expressed by women in this study indicated that reforms are urgently needed at all levels of the criminal justice system. To begin with, all police departments should have special training programs on domestic violence. According to the respondents, officers apparently still have a stereotyped view of the abused wife as a woman who stays "because she likes it," and are unsympathetic. Therefore, police officers need to appreciate the fact that there are extenuating circumstances, such as a lack of money or housing, which sometimes influence a woman to stay. In addition, it might be advisable to have a special team to handle domestic disturbances, perhaps including a female officer. The presence of another woman would no doubt be supportive to a victim, particularly if she were traumatized from a recent beating. Second, there must be a greater effort on the part of district attorneys and lawyers to prosecute cases of wife abuse. Wife-beating must be viewed as a crime and prosecuted with as much vigor as any other form of assault. In addition, there is a need to establish advocacy programs with volunteers who provide emotional support to a woman through the long trial process. Third, laws pertaining to domestic violence should be reformed. For example, officers could be given the authority to have a batterer confined for psychiatric observation for a limited time, thereby ensuring the woman's safety for a period. Free from fear, she would be in a better position to make decisions about her future. Laws pertaining to restraining orders also need revision. Until violation of a restraining order is a felony and arrests can be made without the officer having witnessed the violation, restraining orders will offer no real physical protection to women.

Finally, judges should be able to require that batterers seek counseling either before the trial or as the sentence. Many women are reluctant to begin proceedings because, quite simply, they do not want to send their husbands to jail. If more alternatives in sentencing were available, women might be more willing to press charges.

There is also a great need for public education programs aimed at three specific groups. First, the general population must be informed about the extent and nature of domestic violence. Many people may still believe that the battered woman somehow enjoys the abuse, and is therefore undeserving of aid.

Second, battered women themselves need to be reached through churches, counseling agencies, public services, and the media. Victims of wife abuse need to know that they should not feel guilty or embarrassed about their problem, and that there is help available. For example, communities could distribute handbooks which contain information on the myths and stereotypes about wifebeating and also provide phone numbers of shelters, legal aid offices, and other resources.

Third, the batterers must somehow be reached. Men must realize that they have no legal or moral right to abuse their wives. In addition, since abusive men are typically reluctant to seek counseling, the message should be conveyed that it is not weak or unmasculine to get help for this problem. It might be advisable for a local men's service group to undertake such a project and provide male counselors. Staff members of shelters for battered women report that batterers are frequently very skeptical of services associated with women's groups.

Conclusions

1. It is not yet possible to definitively specify any one predisposing variable common to all batterers. Although violent men tended to be less educated than non-violent men, this factor was confounded by status inequality between husband and wife. Violence in the family of origin was also more prevalent among batterers, but it was by no means a necessary factor. Results do suggest, however, that there may be some as yet unidentified element in a man's background which predisposes him to use violence against his wife.

2. Although no one "type" of batterer was found, the man's dominance level was related to the severity of his violence. In addition, it appears that most battered women were low in self-esteem.

3. It may be possible to categorize domestic violence according to whether the man was perceived as using physical force as a means of achieving total domination over his wife or whether the violence was used to achieve specific, limited goals. Men who used violence for total domination require a different type of therapy than men who resort to violence for other reasons.

4. Although the influence of personality factors cannot be discounted, in the present sample violence was best predicted by a combination of these factors: violence in the backgrounds of both the man and woman, status inequality, and heavy alcohol use by the man.

5. Women in this study frequently found that the community response was inadequate. Public policy should be directed toward providing women with some legal means of obtaining protection from a violent spouse, toward simplifying welfare programs, and toward the development of public education projects.

REFERENCES

Adams, J. Letter to Abigail Adams, April 14, 1776. In L. Butterfield (Ed.), *Adams family correspondence.* Cambridge: Harvard University Press, 1963. Cited in C. Hymowitz and M. Weissman, *A history of women in America.* New York: Bantam Books, 1978.

Alberti, L. (*The family in Renaissance Florence.*) R. Watkins (trans.), University of South Carolina, 1969. Cited in J. O'Faolain and L. Martines (Eds.), *Not in God's image.* New YOrk: Harper and Row, 1973.

Altbach, E. *Women in America.* Lexington: D. C. Heath and Company, 1974.

Andelin, H. *Fascinating womanhood.* New Revised Edition, New York: Bantam Books, 1974.

Bandura, A. *Aggression - a social learning analysis.* Englewood Cliffs: Prentice-Hall, 1973.

Banner, L. *Women in modern America - a brief history.* New York: Harcourt Brace Jovanovich, Inc., 1974.

Barden, J. Wife beaters: few of them ever appear before a court of law. The New York Times, October 21, 1974,

Section 2, p. 38.

Baron, R. A. Magnitude of victim's pain cues and level of prior anger arousal as determinants of adult aggressive behavior. *Journal of Personality and Social Psychology,* 1971, *17*, 236-243.

Book of the knight of la tour-landry. Early English Text Society (1868), 25. Cited in G. Coulton, Medieval panorama, the English scene from conquest to reformation. New York: Meridian Books, 1958.

Borofsky, G., Stollak, G., and Messe, L. Sex differences in bystander reactions to physical assault. *Journal of Experimental Social Psychology,* 1971, 7, 313-318.

Brandwein, R., Brown, C., and Fox, E. Women and children last: the social situation of divorced mothers and their families. *Journal of Marriage and the Family,* August, 1974, *36*, 498-514.

Bucer, De regno Christi, Book 2, Chapter 34. Cited in J. O'Faolain and L. Martines (Eds.) *Not in God's image.* New York: Harper & Row, 1973.

Buss, A. H. Instrumentality of aggression, feedback, and frustration as determinants of physical aggression. *Journal of Personality and Social Psychology*, 1966, *3*, 153-162.

Camden, C. *The Elizabethan woman.* Houston: Elsevier Press, 1952.

Carlson, B. Battered women and their assailants. *Social Work*, November, 1977, 455-460.

Chesler, P. Women as psychiatric and psychotherapeutic patients. *Journal of Marriage and the Family*, November, 1971, 746-759.

Coulton, G. *Medieval panorama, the English scene from conquest to reformation.* New York: Meridian Books, 1955.

Davidson, T. Wifebeating: a recurring phenomenon throughout history. In M. Roy (Ed.), *Battered women - a psychosociological study of domestic violence.* New York: Van Nostrand Reinbold Company, 1977.

Davidson, T. *Conjugal crime - understanding and changing the wifebeating pattern.* New York: Hawthorn Books, Inc., 1978.

Dew, T. Dissertation on the characteristic differences between the sexes, and on the position and influence of women in society. *Southern Literary Messenger,* Richmond, Virginia, I, May 1835, 493-512. In A. Kraditor (Ed.), *Up from the pedestal - selected writings in the history of American feminism.* Chicago: Quadrangle Books, 1968.

Fasteau, M. Why aren't we talking? In J. Pleck and J. Sawyer (Eds.), *Men and masculinity.* Englewood Cliffs: Prentice-Hall, Inc.

Freud, S. (Some psychical consequences of the anatomical distinction between the sexes.) In J. Strachey (Ed. and trans.), The standard edition of the complete psychological works of Sigmund Freud, Vol. XIX. London: The Hogarth Press, 1961.

Friedan, B. *The feminine mystique.* New Dell Edition, New

York: Dell Publishing Company, 1974.

Gayford, J. Wife battering: a preliminary survey of 100 cases. *British Medical Journal*, January, 1975, 194-197.

Gelles, R. *The violent home - a study of physical aggression between husbands and wives.* Beverly Hills: Sage Publications, 1972.

Gies, F., and Gies, J. *Women in the Middle Ages.* New York: Thomas Y. Crowell Company, 1978.

Goldstein, J. H., Davis, R., & Herman, D. Escalation of aggression: experimental studies. *Journal of Personality and Social Psychology*, 1975, *31*, 162-170.

Hartley, R. Sex-role pressures in the socialization of the male child. In J. Pleck and J. Sawyer (Eds.) *Men and masculinity.* Englewood Cliffs: Prentice-Hall, Inc., 1974.

Hilberman, E. and Munson, K. Sixty battered women. *Victimology*, 1977-78, Vol. 2., *314*, 460-471.

Holy Bible, Revised Standard Version. New York: Thomas Nelson and Sons, 1952.

Hymowitz, C. & Weissman, M. *A history of women in America.* New York: Bantam Books, 1978.

Jouard, S. *The transparent self.* Princeton: Van Nostrand Press, 1964.

Kramer H. and Sprenger, J. (*Malleus maleficarum.*) In M. Summers (trans.), Arrow Books, Ltd., 1971. Cited in J. O'Faolain and L. Martines (Eds.), *Not in God's image.* New York: Harper and Row, 1973.

Langley, R. and Levy, R. *Wife beating - the silent crisis.* New York: Simon and Shuster, 1978.

Larwood, L. and Wood, M. *Women in management.* Lexington: D. C. Heath and Company, 1977.

Levinson, D. and Huffman, P. Traditional family ideology and its relation to personality. *Journal of Personality*, 1954-55, *23*, 251-273.

London, J. Images of violence against women. *Victimology*, 1977-78, Vol. 2, No. 3/4, 510-524.

Lundberg, F., and Farnham, M. *Modern woman - the lost sex.* New York: Harper & Brothers Publishing, 1947.

Luther, M. (The table talk.) In T. Tappert (Ed. and trans.), *Luther's works*, Vol. LIV, Philadelphia, 1967. Cited in J. O'Faolain and L. Martines (Eds.), *Not in God's image.* New York: Harper & Row, 1973.

Maccoby, E., and Jacklin, C. *The psychology of sex differences.* Stanford University Press, 1974.

Martin, D. *Battered wives.* San Francisco: Glide Publications, 1976.

Moebius, P. Concerning the physiological and intellectual weakness of women. Cited in B. Ehrenreich and D. English, *Complaints and disorders - the sexual politics of sickness.* Old Westbury: The Feminist Press, Glass Mountain Pamphlet No. 2, 1973.

Morgan, M. *The total woman.* Paperback Edition, New York: Simon and Schuster, 1973.

O'Brien, J. Violence in divorce - prone families. *Journal of Marriage and the Family*, 1971, *33*, 692-698.

O'Neill, W. *Everyone was brave - the rise and fall of feminism in America.* Chicago: Quadrangle Books, 1969.

Paolo da Certaldo. (Libro di buoni costumi.) A. Schiaffini (Ed. and trans.), Florence, 1945. Cited in J. O'Faolain and L. Martines (Eds.), *Not in God's image.* New York: Harper & Row, 1973.

Parker, E., and Schumacher, D. The battered wife syndrome and violence in the nuclear family of origin: a controlled pilot study. *American Journal of Public Health*, 1977, *67*, 760-761.

Prescott, S. and Letko, C. Battered women - a social psychological perspective. In M. Roy (Ed.), *Battered women - a psychosociological study of domestic violence.* New York: Van Nostrand Reinbold Company, 1977, 72-96.

Roy, M. A current survey of 150 cases. In M. Roy (Ed.), *Battered women - a psychosociological study of domestic violence.* New York: Van Nostrand Reinbold Company, 1977, 25-44.

Scott, P. Battered wives. *British Journal of Psychiatry*, 1974, 125, 433-441.

Stark, R. and McEvoy, J. Middle class violence. *Psychology Today*, November, 1970, 52-54; 110-112.

Stern, P. The womanly image: character assassination through the ages. In C. Adams & M. Briscoe (Eds.), *Up against the wall, mother. . .on women's liberation.* Beverly Hills, Glencoe Press, 1971.

Straus, M. Wife beating: how common and why? *Victimology*, 1977,78, Vol. 2, *3-4*, 443-457.

Symonds, A. Violence against women: the myth of masochism. *American Journal of Psychotherapy*, April, 1979, Vol. 33, *2*, 161-173.

Taylor, S. P., and Epstein, S. Aggression as a function of the interaction of the sex of the aggressor and the sex of the victim. *Journal of Personality*, 1967, *35*, 474-486.

Walker, L. *The battered woman*. New York: Harper and Roy, 1979.

Reference Notes

1. Churchill & Strauss, M. Unpublished manuscript.*
2. Walton, M. Personal communication, May 2, 1979.
3. Leech, J. Personal communication, April 8, 1979.
4. Leech, J. Personal communication, April 8, 1979.
5. Walton, M. Personal communication, May 4, 1979.
6. Leech, J. Personal communication, April 8, 1979.
7. Leech, J. Personal communication, April 8, 1979.
8. Walton, M. Personal communication, May 2, 1979.
9. Walton, M. Personal communication, May 2, 1979.
10. Flemming, A. Battered women: issues of public policy. A consultation sponsored by the United States Commission on Civil Rights, Washington, D.C., January 30-31, 1978.
11. Bustus, K. Personal communication, May 10, 1979.
12. Bustus, K. Personal communication, May 10, 1979.
13. Bustus, K. Personal communication, May 10, 1979.
14. Calzaretta, R. Personal communication, June 14, 1979.
15. Friedman, C. Personal communication, June 2, 1979.
16. Leech, J. Personal communication, April 8, 1979.
17. Walton, M. Personal communication, May 4, 1979.
18. Walton, M. Personal communication, May 4, 1979.
19. Walton, M. Personal communication, May 4, 1979.
20. Benton, R. & Wichman, H. Escalation of aggression. Unpublished manuscript, Claremont Men's College, 1979.
21. Benton, R. & Wichman, H. Escalation of aggression. Unpublished manuscript, Claremont Men's College, 1979.
22. Benton, R. & Wichman, H. Escalation of aggression. Unpublished manuscript, Claremont Men's College, 1979.

*No title, date, or other information was provided in the primary source.

Footnotes

[1]Primary source not presently available.

[2]Primary source not presently available

[3]Primary source not given.

[4]Primary source not given.

[5]Information on primary source is incomplete.

[6]Primary source not given.

[7]Primary source not given.

[8]Primary source not given.

[9]Information on primary source is incomplete.

[10]Primary source not given.

[11]Primary source not given.

[12]Primary source not given.

[13]Information on primary source is incomplete.

[14]Ms. Walton, M.S.W., is a consultant to several alcoholism programs and shelters for battered women.

[15]Ms. Leech is a counselor at Haven House, a shelter for battered women.

[16]All references are based on the author's experiences

as a counselor on a local hot-line for battered women.

[17]Ms. Bustus is an Assistant District Attorney for San Bernardino County.

[18]House of Ruth is an organization which operates a hot-line for battered women.

[19]Ms. Friedman is a counselor at Haven House.

[20]Information on primary source is incomplete.

[21]No primary source given.

[22]Although arrangements had been made for that interview, the woman's husband, from whom she was currently separated, had disabled her car. By the time she was recontacted, the car was again in working order, but her husband had recently threatened to kill her and anyone who tried to help her. Since he owned several guns, the woman felt that meeting in person would represent a substantial risk to us both.

[23]Men who were less violent were also often jealous and insecure. The terms are included in the profile in order to present a more complete description.

APPENDIX

Interview Schedule

1. Could you please tell me about the violence in your marriage/relationship?

   Probe questions - Set 1 and Set 2

2. Is there anything else you would like to add that would help us understand the violence in your marriage/relationship?

Probe Questions - Set 1

Variables Relating to Specific Violent Incidents:

When did the first incident occur?
Was beating preceded by verbal argument? If so, about what?
Was a weapon used? If so, what?
Was he intoxicated? On drugs?
Had she been drinking? On drugs?
Were there any witnesses?
Did she fight back? If so, what effect did it have?
Did the violence escalate during the episode?
Did she know what he wanted from her, i.e., what he hoped

to accomplish by the beating?
What caused him to stop?
Were the police called?
Did anyone else (children, neighbors, etc.) try to intervene? If so, what effect did this have?
Did she see a doctor afterwards?
Did she go to a hospital?
Did the violence increase in frequency and/or severity over time?
Was there a discernible pattern to the beatings, that is, could she predict them?

Probe Questions - Set 2

Questions Related to Environmental Conditions:

Was he employed at the time?
Was she?
Was husband having problems with his job?
Were they having any financial difficulties? Who handled the money?
Was she pregnant?
How many children did they have?
Were there any other stressful conditions at the time (i.e., death in the family, birth of child, prolonged illness, etc.)?
Did they have many friends?
Did they socialize much?
Did they have relatives living nearby?

Questions Related to the Couple's Reaction to the Violence:

How did she feel after the episode?
Did she tell anyone about it? If so, whom? What was their reaction? If not, why didn't she?
Did she discuss incident with husband? Was he remorseful?

In what way, if any, did her feelings and behavior toward her husband change?

Did he want to have sexual intercourse after the beating? If so, what do you think was his motivation?

How did children react to the violence? Did she ever discuss incidents with them?

What did she think he was trying to accomplish by being violent?

General Information and Background;

Was her husband abused as a child? What was the relationship with his parents like?

Were his parents violent?

Did she have violent parents? What was her childhood like?

Was she physically or sexually abused as a child?

What were/are the occupations of her father and father-in-law?

How does she describe her husband's personality?

Was husband a jealous person?

QUESTIONNAIRE A

If you have ever had any contact with any of these agencies, please rate your experience with them;

DPSS (Welfare)
___Complete satisfaction
___Moderate satisfaction
___Moderate dissatisfaction
_✓_Complete dissatisfaction

Police
_✓_Complete satisfaction
___Moderate satisfaction
___Moderate dissatisfaction
___Complete dissatisfaction

Pastor
___Complete satisfaction
___Moderate satisfaction
___Moderate dissatisfaction
___Complete dissatisfaction

Lawyer
___Complete satisfaction
___Moderate satisfaction
___Moderate dissatisfaction
___Complete dissatisfaction

Psychiatrist
___Complete satisfaction
___Moderate satisfaction
___Moderate dissatisfaction
___Complete dissatisfaction

Psychologist (Counselor)
___Complete satisfaction
___Moderate satisfaction
___Moderate dissatisfaction
___Complete dissatisfaction

Physician (If consulted for injuries due to battering)
_✓_Complete satisfaction
___Moderate satisfaction
___Moderate dissatisfaction
___Complete dissatisfaction

Social Worker
___Complete satisfaction
_✓_Moderate satisfaction
___Moderate dissatisfaction
___Complete dissatisfaction

QUESTIONNAIRE B

1. A child should not be allowed to talk back to his parents, or else he will lose respect for them.

___Strongly Agree
___Agree
_✓_Disagree
___Strongly Disagree
___Undecided

2. A well-raised child is one who doesn't have to be told twice to do something.

___Strongly Agree
___Agree
___Disagree
_✓_Strongly Disagree
___Undecided

3. If children are told too much about sex, they are likely to go too far in experimenting with it.

___Strongly Agree
___Agree
_✓_Disagree
___Strongly /Disagree
___Undecided

4. Whatever some educators say, "Spare the rod and spoil the child" still holds, even in these modern times.

___Strongly Agree
___Agree
___Disagree
_✓_Strongly Disagree
___Undecided

5. A man can scarceley maintain respect for his fiancee if they have sexual relations before they are married.

___Strongly Agree
___Agree
___Disagree
_✓_Strongly Disagree
___Undecided

6. It goes against nature to place women in positions of authority over men.

___Strongly Agree
_✓_Agree
___Disagree
___Strongly Disagree
___Undecided

7. Women have as much right as men to sow wild oats.
   _✓_Strongly Agree   ___Disagree
   ___Agree   ___Strongly Disagree
                  ___Undecided

8. Women who want to remove the word *obey* from the marriage ceremony don't understand what it means to be a wife.
   ___Strongly Agree   ___Disagree
   ___Agree   _✓_Strongly Disagree
                  ___Undecided

9. Some equality in marriage is a good thing, but by and large the husband ought to have the main say-so in family matters.
   ___Strongly Agree   ___Disagree
   ___Agree   _✓_Strongly Disagree
                  ___Undecided

QUESTIONNAIRE C

Section 1

Please rate the amount you have told your husband/living partner about these matters. In rating, please consider the whole time you have been married/living together.

0	I have told him nothing about this
1	I have told him only general things about this
2	I have talked about this in full and complete detail
X	I have lied or misrepresented myself to him about this

Items

_2_ 1. Things in the past or present that I feel ashamed and guilty about

_0_ 2. Whether or not I feel that I am attractive to the opposite sex

_0_ 3. What it takes to make me very worried, anxious and afraid

_0_ 4. What it takes to make me feel very depressed or blue

_0_ 5. What it takes to hurt my feelings deeply

_0_ 6. The kinds of things that make me especially proud of myself

_0_ 7. Whether or not he is able to satisfy me sexually

_0_ 8. What things really make me angry

_0_ 9. What feelings, if any, I have trouble expressing

____ 10. What feelings, if any, I have trouble controlling

Section 2

Please rate how much you think your husband/living partner has told *you* about these matters:

__2__ 1. Things in the past or present that he feels ashamed and guilty about

__2__ 2. Whether or not he feels that he is attractive to the opposite sex

__2__ 3. What it takes to make him very worried, anxious and afraid

__2__ 4. What it takes to make him feel very depressed or blue

__2__ 5. What it takes to hurt his feelings deeply

__2__ 6. The kinds of things that make him especially proud of himself

__2__ 7. Whether or not I am able to satisfy him sexually

__2__ 8. What things really make him angry

__2__ 9. What feelings, if any, he has trouble expressing

__2__ 10. What feelings, if any, he has trouble controlling